How to Outsmart the New Car Salesman

How to Outsmart the New Car Salesman

GARY CARR

COLLIER BOOKS
MACMILLAN PUBLISHING COMPANY
New York

COLLIER MACMILLAN PUBLISHERS
London

Copyright © 1987 by Gary Carr

Macmillan Publishing Company
866 Third Avenue, New York, N.Y. 10022

Library of Congress Cataloging-in-Publication Data

Carr, Gary.
How to outsmart the new car salesman.

Includes index.
1. Automobiles—Purchasing.   I. Title.
TL162.C396   1987   629.2′222′029   87-11616
ISBN 0-02-018290-2

Macmillan books are available at special discounts for bulk purchases for sales promotions, premiums, fund-raising, or educational use. For details, contact:
Special Sales Director
Macmillan Publishing Company
866 Third Avenue
New York, N.Y. 10022

10   9   8   7   6   5   4   3   2   1

Printed in the United States of America

To the three women in my life

To my mother, Inez, who has waited a long time to see me finally achieve one of my lifelong dreams.

To my daughter, Christine, who can now be proud of something her father has accomplished, and who never lost faith in me.

To my girlfriend, Sharon, who in all the years of knowing me has never stopped believing in me or caring for me. And who taught me that real success is having someone to care for and who cares for you in return.

Acknowledgments

I would like to thank my agent, Ms. Carol Mann, for having the foresight and the wisdom to help me pursue my goal in the publishing of this book. Also, thanks to Mr. Barry Lippman and Mr. David Wolff of Macmillan for thinking that what I had to say was important enough to publish.

Contents

. . . .

Some Straight Talk
About the Car Business

So, you want to save a lot of money on your next vehicle purchase. Doesn't everyone? And you think that simply by reading this book, you'll be able to do exactly that. Well, you're absolutely right. But before we begin, I'm going to help you get to the real Bottom Line, by telling you a few startling facts about the automobile industry.

Fact: Over twenty million people will purchase a new vehicle during the coming model year.

Fact: Thirty million more Americans next year will try unsuccessfully to buy a vehicle.

Fact: The automobile manufacturers and dealers will spend over one billion advertising dollars in an attempt to lure unsuspecting and inexperienced shoppers into showrooms during the current model run.

Fact: The manufacturers and the dealers together spend millions each year on complex training programs that are designed to do just one thing: ensure that their salespeople have the best skills and knowledge possible, as well as the best support systems available, in order to maintain the highest volume of sales and the largest profits possible.

Fact: A professional automobile salesman sells vehicles 365 days a year, while a car buyer only makes a purchase once every four or five years. How can the customer ever hope to compete against such odds?

Fact: Millions of dollars are spent each year by the factories as well as the dealers on sales promotional contests. Trips to Bermuda, Europe, and the Orient are commonplace. These trips are financed with the money from the profits of the sale of cars and trucks.

Fact: Look around. Dealerships are becoming bigger, more luxurious, and much more prosperous at the expense of the American car buyer. The last two energy crises have forced a lot of smaller dealerships out of business. The result is that with fewer dealers and less competition, profits are dramatically higher.

Fact: Today, more than ever before, the multiline car dealer is fast becoming the monster of the midway. When a dealer handles more than one brand of car or truck, he has a better chance to sell you something. After several hours of looking at different varieties of vehicles, many customers are just too tired to say "no" to an aggressive professional salesperson. Customers feel that if they must go through this agonizing ordeal each time they drive onto a lot, they might as well surrender right now. Many do exactly that.

Fact: When a dealer carries more than one brand of vehicle, his profits are greater yet. The reason is lower overhead: he employs only one office staff, one management staff, one group of detail guys, one group of service writers and mechanics, and one bunch of talented and well-trained salespeople.

Fact: Since 1980 the manufacturers have pulled off one of the biggest cons in history. Due to the continual increase in the already high sticker prices affixed to the windows of new cars, customers would get sticker shock each time they walked into a showroom. The public was not going to take it anymore. So the factories simply reduced the markup on the vehicles from an average of 18 to 24 percent to the present markups of 10 to 15 percent. This maneuver cut hundreds of dollars from the MSRP (manufacturer's suggested retail price), which gave the illusion of price reduction. On Monday a new Chevy Monte Carlo might have been priced at $12,000 and on Tuesday the same vehicle might have been $11,214 after the reduction of markup. The price seemed to have been drastically reduced, but in fact all that was given up was the dealer's excess discount. Yes, I said discount. Remember years ago when the dealers would let you have a healthy discount for some important reason, like you're paying cash, or it's a sunny day today, or you're the first sale of the day. The salespeople would give you a discount for just about any reason. (And you thought you had been so clever to negotiate that by yourself.) Now, in the era of reduced markup, the dealers had to somehow regain their profits. So we saw the invention of the supplementary sticker affixed next to the MSRP label required by the EPA. This new sticker listed all the dealer-installed items, such as paint protection, rustproofing, vinyl roof, sun roof, and radio, that could be installed at low cost by the service department and could be marked up by several hundred percent. Therefore, a large discount could still be given (when necessary) without damaging dealer profits.

Fact: Today's car buyers have little or no chance of making a good deal. They are not equipped with the knowledge or training to compete with a professional salesperson. The more consumer-oriented our society becomes, the sharper its salespeople become. Slick sales training programs and sales seminars are an on-going fact of life. These highly successful classes exist for the sole purpose of generating more sales at higher profits.

Fact: Many publications list prices of vehicles and "extras," right down to the freight charges. However, when you visit a new-car showroom with price book in hand, a real professional will tell you to ask the publisher of the price book to get you the vehicle at a lower price. As long as you buy here, you will pay what my manager says you pay or you simply can't buy here. What do you do then?

Fact: There are literally hundreds of books offered to the sales managers and salespeople that cover everything from closing deals to overcoming consumer resistance. The material is there for the asking. Audio and video presentations allow entire sales departments to view or listen; nothing is overlooked by a good manager and sales staff. There are even men and women who travel the country and lecture exclusively on how to sell, motivate your customers, and increase profits.

Fact: In a showroom you are up against the most talented and the most experienced salespeople that the dealer can assemble. Managers with years of experience in training and developing people, salespeople with hundreds of sales under their belts, and everyone employed by the dealer are there for one reason only—to sell you a vehicle at the highest possible price.

Now, are you ready to walk into a dealership, stroll up to a sales rep, and begin to talk turkey?

YES, as soon as you finish reading this book.

I hope to give you the training, the motivation, and the firepower so that a professional automobile salesperson will never again take unfair advantage of you and your family. You work hard for your money and there is no reason to let someone take it from you. The next time you walk into a showroom you're going to have the peace of mind that comes from the knowledge that you won't get ripped off. More important, you'll have the edge on your opponent. He will not know that you know what he knows! You will even be familiar with the car lingo used by many of the pros in the business. By the time this book gets around to the dealers and they read it, I'll need a bodyguard and you'll know all the secrets of the car business.

Assuming that you still want to save a great deal of money, I think that the time has come to get to the bottom line. Don't you agree?

How to Outsmart the New Car Salesman

Who and What Are You Up Against?

Each year millions of Americans contemplate the purchase of new and used motor vehicles. Typical American car or truck buyers will not only walk into dealerships across the United States grossly unprepared, but will actually believe that they are going to beat a professional automobile salesperson at his or her own game, the complicated and frustrating game of cars.

That is, a car buyer who makes a purchase once every three or four years goes up against an organization of trained professionals who sell vehicles each and every day of the year, and expects to win. Can you, as a person who has spent thousands of hard-earned dollars on vehicles over the years, honestly look at yourself in the mirror and say that you were not terrified when you finally said yes and bought your last car or truck? How confident were you that you had made the best deal possible?

Don't kid yourself

In fact, you hadn't a clue as to how much profit the dealer and his crew made on you. You had a nice salesperson, who had your best interests at heart, right? You probably went to the dealership not to buy but just to look. Then you met a guy or gal who really made you feel comfortable and had a ton of old-fashioned personality. You said to yourself, this dealership is sure a lot better than some of the others in the area.

Folks, you simply ran into a real salesman. I wish I had a dollar for each time I heard a customer tell me that he had no intention of purchasing a car that day. Or that he felt sorry for poor old Bill, the salesman, and decided to buy a car to make him feel better (the old guilt routine). The last thing a good salesperson will do when he is having no success is to put you on a guilt trip. "Golly, Mr. and Mrs. Jones, I'm sure sorry that I took up two hours of your valuable time, and I'm sorry we can't seem to get together on the price today. It's surely the best deal in town. I don't ever remember our sales manager going that low on this car. Wait, I'll bet it's me. I must have done something to offend you. What is it? Tell me so I won't do it again to any future customers. Please tell me what I've done wrong before my manager asks me why you didn't buy. I'm afraid that as soon as it comes out—whatever your reason for not buying—he will fire me. Both of us know that it can't possibly be the price. So he'll figure I did something to make you mad."

It only takes a minute or two for a good grinder to put you on the guilt trip of your life. After all, you've just spent two or three hours with him and by now you both know a great deal about each other. At least he knows a great deal about you. He was listening to every word you said, but were you listening to him or looking at all the shiny new cars? A good salesperson always is a great listener. And what do we like to talk about the most? Right—ourselves!

First, we try to show a salesperson that we're tough, hard, fearless. We tell him war stories about our last purchase and how we made the dealer fall to his knees and beg us to buy. Then we tell our astute peddler just how we plan to do this deal today. We tell him that we won't be buying until we check prices in at least three other agencies. We tell him that we are, indeed, just looking. But then a subtle question from our sales pro sends us to new heights of stupidity. "Gee, Mr. Jones, I see that no one is going to take advantage of you. You must really be a successful person to have this much self-control. I sure hope that some day I can be as tough as you. By the way, where did you buy your last car?" That sounds harmless enough, right? Wrong!

Can you figure out eight reasons the above sales pitch is effective?

1. "Gee" plants the seed of the sales rep's down-home honesty and simplicity in the customer's mind.

2. The compliment about being successful boosts the customer's ego, thus relieving him of any further need to prove himself to the sales rep.

3. "Can't take advantage of you" lulls the customer to sleep because the sales rep seems to have made a concession.

4. "Self-control" also gives the customer a false sense of security.

5. The wish to be "as tough as you some day" will destroy any real defenses the customer has left. Now all the rep must do is overcome the fact that the customer is now simply on guard.

6. The word "tough" lets the customer believe that the rep knows he's a tough guy.

7. The answer to the question "Where did you buy your last car?" tells the rep the name of the dealer, which will enable him to figure out how hard to "grind" on his customer. Dealers have reputations with the sales reps

who sell in the same area. If a particular agency has the dubious honor of being one of the "TO" houses in the community, then the rep will know how the customer is accustomed to be treated. Or if the last dealer just happens to be a competitor, it helps the manager to determine the potential profit margin or at least what to shoot for. All good managers know, within about a hundred dollars, just how much their counterparts are charging for any model.

8. The answer will inform the rep when the buyer bought last. This helps the manager because he may be able to determine under what sales system the buyer purchased his present car. Everyone had a system then, and everyone has a system now. (Sales systems will be explained in Chapters 3 and 4.)

And you thought buying a car was easy. It is easy if you follow the smooth road on which the rep is leading you. However, the more bumps you introduce, the better you'll like the deal you end up making.

Customers *always* underestimate their sales reps, and they *grossly* underestimate them. It is important that you understand that statement.

Chapter 3 in this book will discuss in detail the various mind games which go on from the time you set foot on the lot until the time you leave. But, to give you an idea of what is to come, permit me to elaborate on one intriguing game that takes place early in the war of wits.

Too often, customers will pull onto the lot, get out of the car, and head immediately to the vehicle that attracts them most. Meanwhile, since most automobile sales forces are on some type of gentleman's arrangement or **up system,*** your rep has already been chosen for you. This professional will usually allow you a minute or two to browse before introducing himself and welcoming you to

* For definitions of terms in boldface, see the Glossary.

the car store. As you gaze at the rows of brand-new cars or trucks, the furthest thing from your mind is the car you drove up in. The pro, who looked you over as you drove in, watches as you jump from your vehicle and proceed to the new car of your dreams. Since you are going to be greeted by this person, and no one else will be allowed to approach you, he can give you as much or as little time as he wants. He can observe you as you browse and see if you are becoming impatient and require assistance or still need more time to look.

As he watches, he casually strolls by your vehicle, which he assumes will be part of the negotiations. In one pass the pro can determine several things. First, if your vehicle is clean, especially on the inside, you probably have decided to trade it and have already removed all personal items. Second, he notices if the license plates are going to expire within the next forty-five days. This is another good indicator of your plans to trade it in. Third, he looks for business cards and/or brochures from other agencies on the front seat. If you have them, the cards may give a clue as to what you may have been offered elsewhere. The fourth item is the overall condition of the vehicle. Will he be able to criticize it because it needs body work? If so, he will offer you less money. Remember, he has already appraised your vehicle's approximate value; now he is merely fine-tuning his evaluation before he greets you.

Try to act like the salesman for a moment. A man and wife pull onto the lot driving a four- or five-year-old vehicle that needs new tires, a new windshield, and maybe a good cleanup. Furthermore, the car is devoid of all valuables inside, and brochures from another agency lie on the front seat. Your customers go immediately to a particular car and are still gazing at it. You've got a good idea of the value of the trade vehicle. As you approach your customers, you see that their strong interest in this car continues. As a pro, you know that you've got a real buyer who's here right now, who went to another dealership and didn't buy there. You've determined all this and have yet to say hello to your customer. Who has the upper hand even before you meet? Who will know instantly which way to go? Who will know if you're telling a white lie if you say yes to the question, is this the first place you've shopped? (Customers usually say that this is the first place even if it is the fiftieth because they fear that other questions may follow as to why they didn't buy elsewhere.)

Now, you, as the sales rep, who knows that the customer has been shopping elsewhere and didn't buy, can now approach the buyer with confidence. "Good afternoon. Welcome to Hometown Motors. My name is Mr. Pro, and I'm glad you're here. How may Hometown Motors be of service to you good people today?" As soon as your customers open their mouths, they will add a great deal of information, all of which will aid you in selling a car for the highest possible price. Pity the poor customer who gets a salesman who has just sold a car and is trying to sell number two or three. He will give a new meaning to the word *aggressive!* Were you as a customer ever in a similar situation? Do you see how simple it is to outgun and outmaneuver an unsuspecting buyer?

Experience is your real enemy

The fact that you are intelligent and dynamic should not be discounted. I am certain that whatever you do for a living, you do it to the very best you can. There may not be many others who can perform your job as well as you do. A salesman or saleswoman who sells cars or trucks for a living is no different from you—with one small exception. If they don't sell you a car, they don't eat or have a roof over their head. A commission sales job is far different from one where you put in your time and collect a paycheck. In sales meetings held by yours truly, I would tell my reps that if they couldn't make it in the car business, they could always become a doctor or lawyer. However, if they wanted to make some real money, they could put their minds to becoming the best salesperson possible. Study the product, know when to talk, go to sales seminars, read, listen, watch your fellow reps, and learn from your mistakes. Fortunately, people buy cars every day and all car salesmen and women get to practice what they do best, every day of the year. As a result many of them become very good at selling. They get to practice on you, the car buyer. It's you who will give them the experience they require to become sales pros. But, you say, how can I ever hope to win at this game of cars? You win by studying your opponent and knowing his attitudes, knowing what he's up to, knowing what his next moves will be, and knowing just how to counteract anything he may try. The money you ultimately save if you can accomplish this task could well be in the hundreds or thousands on your next purchase.

Save $10,000 over a lifetime

Reading this book will help you save a minimum of $500 on each vehicle you purchase for the rest of your life. Depending on the number of cars you buy, that's a possible savings of $10,000. Just think, if you saved ten thousand dollars or more on your vehicle purchases, what a tidy sum you would have collecting interest in your savings account.

Presenting the players

To understand what you're up against when you purchase a car or truck, it is vital to know who you will be dealing with. We've discussed some of the attitudes; now we must talk about some of the people who are involved before we continue.

The manufacturers

General Motors, Ford, Chrysler, Toyota, Nissan, and the rest all have one goal. It is not what you may think, however. They sell vehicles to the dealerships of the world and *not* to you, the buying public. Although you, as an individual buyer, are extremely important to them, their main concern is the group of dealers that represents them. The number of car sales over any given period is not based upon what the public buys, but rather upon how many vehicles the dealers order and receive. When you read in the newspaper that car sales are up or down by 10 percent over the past year, the figures do not refer to cars sold to you, but to the dealers.

This is where the game gets interesting. When the cars are simply not moving off the dealers' lots, screams are heard far and wide by everybody from the large dealerships to government officials, from banks and finance companies to union leaders. Soon the factories bail everyone out by creating some sort of incentive program that will induce people to come out and buy now. This being the case, it makes no sense at all even to think about making a car purchase without having a nondealer-participation incentive offered by the factory through which you intend to purchase a vehicle.

Dealer participation may affect the price you pay

Most "rebates" offered by the factories do indeed affect the price of the vehicle you buy. The manufacturer may feel generous and offer you a thousand-dollar rebate on a particular car or truck. However, since there is no "free lunch," the factory tells its dealers that should they wish to participate, each car or truck sold while the rebate is running will cost the dealer a certain sum, for example, $250. This amount is the dealer portion of the rebate and is deducted by the factory from the dealer's account. But guess who really pays the dealer's portion of the rebate? You got it—the buyer. The next question out of your mouth should be, "But is that fair?" The answer . . . is yes. Even though *you* really end up paying the dealer portion, you still net $750, which is quite respectable. You will get a check for $1000, but all the dealer did was mark up his vehicle by $250 to cover his share. So the bottom line on "rebates" is to use them. Make your best deal, and then wait for your check.

Lower interest rates are the best inducement

The most popular way of getting customers to flock to dealer showrooms is to reduce finance or interest rates and charges. Usually the manufacturer already has its own finance house, such as General Motors Acceptance Corporation (GMAC) or Ford Motor Credit Corporation (FMCC) or Chrysler Credit Corporation, which will simply offer cut-rate financing in the hope that, lower rates producing lower payments, more people will be able to afford a new vehicle. This is a genuine opportunity for consumers to save hundreds of dollars. The financial institution will make a smaller return on the investment, and the vehicle is quickly sold —the real object of the entire exercise.

But they still gotcha

Even though both kinds of offers are attractive, the factories and dealers still play the game to suit themselves. You will note that these offers are always limited to specific models, which may not include the one you wish to purchase. In recent years the factories have specified not only the car they want you to buy but the engine as well. If that car is one that you can live with, you're in luck. If not, then wait for three or four months for the next giveaway to occur and you will see a new set of cars or trucks. If you have a little patience, you can save a small fortune in finance charges. Too often we tend to do what people around us are doing. Our friends, neighbors, or co-workers go out and make a deal, and we feel that if we don't act now, we'll lose the chance of a lifetime. Just wait. Stand your ground and soon an even better deal will be out there.

Caution, caution, caution

It seems as though the more the factories try to create business through offering good deals, the more some dealers attempt to take advantage of them. What such dealers practice is legal, but to an unsuspecting buyer it could prove to be a lethal blow. **Buying down an interest rate,** for example, one of the biggest con games going, is used to bring buyers, not lookers, to the lot. Did you ever notice that certain dealerships in your area always seem to advertise super low interest rates on many of their vehicles? I'm referring to 4 percent or 6 percent APR, whichever will get your attention. The ad implies that buyers receive some sort of specially arranged bank rate. For a limited time, such as during a special ten-day sales event or holiday sale, the lucky buyer can get this great APR.

Let's assume the normal bank rate is 13 percent APR and the dealer wants to offer the public 4 percent APR for a specific sale. The dealer must pay the difference between the rates, in this case 9 percent, to pay the lender if this arrangement is to work. The catch is that the term or length of time one can finance a vehicle under an ultra-low rate such as this is generally limited to twenty-four or thirty months, which almost always makes the monthly payments too high for many people. Customers on a budget or fixed income always get sucked in by these low rates. When they get to the real bottom line, these people are forced to switch to longer terms at a higher rate of interest, in order to make the payments fit their own specific needs.

Now I hope the question of where the dealer gets all the money to pay that 9 percent difference between rates has been burning a hole in your pocketbook.

You got it . . . you get to pay it, again!

There is, indeed, a huge sum of money that this wonderful dealer has to pay directly to the bank in order to give you this super rate of interest. You, the buyer, will pay every penny of this difference. You not only have to pay for the car, but you get to pay the bank too. A regular Ford Escort might have an MSRP sticker of $8500, but when the dealer adds the additional markup to cover the difference in finance rates, it could well be at $11,200. Try to ask for a discount, and you'll never get a straight answer. What you will get, however, is a sales rep who has been trained in the art of switching your thinking to monthly payments in lieu of anything else. Go ahead, ask questions, and see what answers you get.

Question: What's my discount going to be?

Answer: What difference does it make as long as your payments are what you can afford? Or, we don't give discounts because of the very low interest. (Buyers will say nothing because they still believe that the interest rate is low enough to justify paying a little more for the car.)

Question: How much are you giving me for my trade?

Answer: What difference does it make as long as you like your monthly payments?

Question: How much an I actually going to pay for the car?

Answer: What difference does it make as long as you can afford the monthly payments?

Get the idea?

Extreme caution, beware, danger!!!

Practically every dealer in the United States employs a highly trained finance or business manager whose everyday job is "selling" dealer financing plans. In addition, these business or finance managers peddle life insurance, health insurance, extended service policies, and even paint protection packages and burglar alarms. Included in the price of each one of these items is a great deal of potential profit for the dealer.

These managers, who are quite often women, actually spend a few weeks each year training at schools that specifically address the selling of financing and related products. They are so rigorously trained that they often give scripts to the salesman designed to "set up" the customer for their financing pitches.

The real trick in being a good finance manager comes after the buyer is sitting in the finance office. The deal has already been made, the figures are on paper, and the buyer has signed. Yes, payments are sometimes quoted, but not always. A good sales rep will always tell his customer not to fret, that the manager will quote the payments, but first we must agree to the deal on paper in order for the finance manager to have some numbers to work with. Sounds fair enough, right? The finance manager must first know how much the customer is paying before he can plug those figures into his computer. Buyer beware. If you do not read the fine print of an ad, then you will be in for the shock of a lifetime. Dealers will rely on the fact that all you will see in the financing offer is the 4 percent APR and *not* that the term is for only twenty-four months. Then when you sit down to finish your deal with the finance manager, who gives you a payment quote more than double what you expected or can afford, you hit the floor. You're too mad to think about anything else but those "damn payments," and you forget all else. When the expert finance man or woman informs you that this special interest rate is available only for those able to pay off the car in just twenty-four months, and hands you a copy of the ad that you have presumably read, you are too embarrassed and nervous about those large payments to think rationally. This is when you should get up and leave. But these people are pros and begin to work hard on you. Your typical first response is "no way, never, forget the deal, I'm not paying that, are you nuts?" Then a calm and collected expert will say, "No problem, we've got the perfect solution. All you have to do is pay the regular bank rate and you then get to finance your vehicle for sixty months instead of twenty-four. Your payments will be cut in half. By the way, Mr. Sucker, if you like, you can pay off your loan early and only be required to pay finance charges for as long as the loan is outstanding and on the books."

Sounds great, right?

In your effort to get out of the dealership, you figure that anything is better than the first payment quote, and by now you've been there for a considerable length of time. You also figure that anywhere else you go will charge the same rate of interest, and you sign your name thinking that after all you've got what you want and that beautiful new car is just waiting out there for you to show off to the whole world. And you just can't wait to "see how she handles." But you forgot one small item. You've just paid $2700 over window sticker for the vehicle and you didn't get that super rate of interest. Or if the payments were not a factor, and you did get the low rate, you paid $2700 over window sticker to do so. (Try to go back to the dealer to see if he will take the car back and stop the transaction and you'll fully understand the meaning of the words, *get out!)*

Stick to factory-authorized deals only

The factory offers are both good and legitimate and will not usually harm you. Make sure you read all the fine print and that the vehicle you buy is the vehicle you want, not one that you feel you "ought" to buy because of the special factory incentive price on it. Chances are good that this vehicle is not selling well, and by waiting you'll get an even better deal later on. Never forget, the factories are interested in selling vehicles first, making profits second, and pleasing customers last.

Factories can set trends in a hurry

At the beginning of the model year the factories, dealers, and fleet departments are busy writing and filling orders to the many thousands of true fleet buyers. Car rental companies, large corporations, government agencies, law enforcement, and thousands of others all place orders in the early part of summer in order to enjoy a full year of use. There have been occasions when the factories have filled these orders first, leaving certain models unavailable for weeks or even months. One company I knew ordered seven thousand vehicles at one time. Naturally, these vehicles were built and delivered first, while normal retail customers had to wait for two months. This meant that these particular vehicles were in great demand with little or no supply on hand. You guessed what happened. The prices were driven up because of the small supply while the value of the same car from the previous year was now reduced because over seven thousand of them were dumped all at once on the used-car marketplace.

So if a retail customer had a year-old car of that particular type and was accustomed to trading it in every year, he would have to pay a premium for the new car while taking an abnormal loss on his used one. A vehicle not in good supply early in a model run can only mean one of two bad things. First, it may be going to fleet buyers and, second, a defect might be impeding its full production. In either case, you'll be better off selecting another vehicle instead of buying something you do not like.

Now that you've seen how a good deal at the factory

level can be turned to your disadvantage by the dealer, let's look more closely at the dealer and his staff.

The dealer and his staff

All dealerships are divided into departments, or what I like to call profit centers. Always bear in mind that every area of a dealership is a major profit center. Even the accounting offices and bookkeeping personnel represent profit to a car store. The quicker deals get processed, the quicker dealers get their money and the faster the dealer stops paying interest on its inventory and begins to accrue interest on the profits. You should understand the work of each profit center because often you will be dealing with more than one. Even though your primary contact will be a sales rep, your vehicle will go through nearly every department before it reaches you. When the vehicle hits the ground, shipping and receiving gets it and sends it over to prep who then farms it out to the service department or even an outside company that might be installing equipment at the dealer's request. Then, back to the detail department for cleaning and finally to sales and then to you. As soon as the car hits the ground the first time, it is assigned a stock number and then begins to accrue various charges that are added each time something is done to that vehicle. The price of the car starts increasing each day until it is sold.

Dealer-added options

Dealer-installed options are one of the best ways for a good sales rep and manager to build a greater profit margin into the deal, and you'll hardly ever know about it. That is because most dealers do it and most charge nearly the same price for many of the added options. I've seen customers fight with a sales rep for an hour to get an extra $100 in additional trade allowance and then turn right around and pay $700 for a paint protection package that costs the dealer $50–$75 to install. This includes undercoating, fabric protection for the upholstery, and the exterior paint sealant that prevents the surfaces from fading. Dealers in the habit of installing these paint protection packages (and I would estimate that over 75 percent of dealers do it) will generally retail this glorified wax job for anywhere from $150 to as high as $1000, and even more in some instances. Vinyl roofs, radios, special tires and wheels, roll bars for trucks, stripes, moldings, fabric seating—the list is endless—should all be competitively shopped for to insure the best value for your money.

Free wax jobs for the life of your car!

If a customer decides not to purchase a paint protection package and saves the $700, he could get a professional job for about $75 performed on his car twice a year for the next four years and still have a hundred bucks left over for dinner and a show. And if you spent a Sunday afternoon on your car or truck two times a year, then that $700 could pay for anything else you need. Even if you have to wait a month or two in order to get that special radio installed, and end up listening to yourself hum your favorite songs, it's well worth getting a better radio from a specialty store, and besides, you'll be financing less so your payments will be lower. You do not want to pay interest on a radio or other accessory for the life of your contract or until you trade the vehicle, do you? Do some homework and find out what these items really cost before you have the dealer install them for you. Shop around; spend some time instead of money for a change.

Who manages these profit centers?

All profit centers of a dealership have the best managers that money can buy. If a manager puts together several bad months in a row, out he goes and fresh talent arrives on the scene. You could say that a manager, especially a sales manager, is like a gunfighter in the Old West. There's always someone out there who says he is better and can't wait to prove it. The law in these parts is the dealer, or general manager, and you can rest assured that it won't be long before someone, eager to rise to the top, takes a shot at the manager. It's the survival of the fittest or the one who, month in and month out, makes the dealer the most profit. We will get into more detail regarding sales management in Chapters 2 and 3.

The reps—both men and women

If Jack Nicklaus walked up to you and wanted to bet you $10,000 that he could beat you in the game of golf, would you take that bet? Of course not! He's a pro and you have no chance to beat him, let alone give him a good match. The salespeople of today are not only professional, but are the best people that any particular dealer can assemble at the moment. You'll see why later on in this book, but for now let me give you a very vivid example. On the average, I spent less time than most managers in training my sales-people. Fortunately I always seemed to get great people. But when I did hire new people, whether they were expe-rienced or not, I usually spent two solid hours just going over how to greet customers properly when they came on the property. You never get a second chance to make a good first impression, so I made sure that my reps would always begin on a positive note. You should have been there when we discussed closing techniques. That class was ongoing and perpetual. At least three or four hours each week was spent in the class, along with countless hours of individual counseling, not to mention the other training programs offered by special motivators who travel around the country as well as a training seminar offered through the factory several times a year.

Firepower

My goal is to give you much of the same firepower that the reps have at their disposal, but in a version that will require you to follow only a few simple steps. I plan to make it fun and exciting for you to make that purchase. After all, it's your money and you've got a right to have some fun with it, don't you?

Since we are on the reps, you might as well know the real bottom line on just what they think of you, the customer, the person who puts a commission in their pockets.

The correct size is needed first

Each time a customer enters the dealership, a dozen sets of eyes immediately focus on that person. Everyone from the reps to the manager to the lot attendants gives the customer the once-over. "He's a flake, he's a looker, here comes a real winner, look at this loser, he couldn't afford to buy the tires let alone the entire car, this guy is a lay-down, here comes a buyer" are some of the words of wisdom that may come out of the mouths of wolves. You are now fair game and each rep is sizing you up. All it will take is just a minute of conversation and the good sales-person will know without any doubt what type you are and if you're a buyer today. Yes, I know you are nervous because you realize everyone has his eye on you. You've only arrived and already you have become intimidated.

What if you were able to size up your sales rep, as he approaches you? I'm sure that possibility is exciting but you don't know where to begin. Well, for now, allow me to explain just what many of the reps think of you. The sales-people, as a general rule, classify customers, and usually right on target. After you read some of the types, see where you are and then, for fun, try to classify some of your friends and neighbors.

The macho male

This is a man who thinks he is the world's best at every-thing he does. He is a know-it-all who will always end up learning the hard way. He'll walk into a dealership, usu-ally with a woman on his arm, and immediately try to impress everyone with his vast knowledge of cars, throw-ing around technical terms and acting as if he knows ex-actly what he wants. Mr. Macho will always spout some ridiculously low offer, assuming that he is overwhelming the rep with his no-nonsense, hard-sell attitude. But just wait until a good rep calls his bluff and says, "OK, you know what you want, let's sit down and hammer out your offer. Put your money where your mouth is." But when Mr. Macho (if he hasn't left the dealership already after having his bluff called) sits down to talk turkey, it be-comes clear that there is little hard knowledge behind his hard-sell front, and the rep will put him through the grinder just like any other customer. And since Mr. Macho wears his classification right on his sleeve, the rep will know just what to say to flatter him, to force him to accept outlandish options in order to impress his ego and his female friend.

So unless you can spot a novice rep who intimidates easily, don't be this type of customer.

The female buyer (single or married)

Some years ago I received a directive from the division whose line of vehicles our store represented that went something like this: henceforth, special attention should be paid to how your staff treats female shoppers and/or buyers. Approximately 60 to 70 percent of the decisions to purchase are made or influenced by women. No longer can successful reps talk only to the male; on the contrary, the female must be drawn into the conversation and be made an important part of the sale. If women play such vital parts in the decision-making process, then we surely must develop new sales presentations that consider the woman for more than picking the color. She will probably help make those monthly payments, too.

Women, take a bow, you've finally got the attention that you rightfully deserve. No longer will you be placed on the back burner when it comes to car sales. You can expect some royal treatment from now on. Notice, I said treatment. I did not say that you would get a good deal just because you're a woman, but that finally you would be treated with a little respect. The attitudes of today's women mean that they will not accept being called "honey," "sweetheart," or "baby doll" any longer by sales reps who are still operating as if it were 1965. Female shoppers are exactly that, shoppers. For the most part, women will generally shop around until they find either a rep who has great knowledge about the product or a great price on the product. In either case, the women will pick up the phone and do some price and product comparing. But, as talented as some women are, they must never forget they are dealing with pros, who in this case have had special training by the dealership and even the factory on just how to handle females. Please don't get upset by this statement. It is intended to let you know just how important your role really is to the sale.

A couple can play havoc with a sales rep if they themselves have a little acting ability. I've seen couples play the "Starsky and Hutch" routine and get away with it. You know, the good guy, bad guy ploy. Usually the man will want the vehicle for the right price, but the woman will insist that the couple continue to shop around for an even better value. This will drive a rep up the wall because he can taste the sale but the woman keeps standing in his way. Just hang in there and be tough. You'll soon see that the "deal" will begin to improve drastically, especially if you hint that one of their competitors is just fifteen minutes away. Suddenly, the pressure will be on to get a commitment from you to buy, but don't do it. Just say, tell me what your best deal is, Mr. Sales Rep, and I'll tell you if it is good enough to earn my business. Yes, the female buyer can be a vital part of a winning combination, if you play the game correctly.

The young couple

Most of the time when young couples enter the dealership, salespeople will attempt to play on their emotions. Two things tend to take place. First, most young people would rather be somewhere else enjoying the good life with their friends than be buying a car. Thus, they tend to act on impulse or on emotion. They usually lead an active life and can only allow an hour or two to complete a transaction that will affect them for the next several years. A pro can generally convince them to go ahead with the deal because it's only money and they should enjoy this wonderful life to the fullest before it's too late. Second, most young men and women believe that they are on their way to success and quickly come to terms with a sharp rep, who continues to tell them how good they will look to their friends when they pull up in that beauty. Who cares if the car is $100 a month more than the budget allows, as long as they look good in it, correct? This must be how part-time jobs were created—by young people biting off more than they can chew and paying for it through additional part-time employment. Young people, take your time! You've got the rest of your life to play, so take enough extra time to get the job done correctly. Don't be another fantastic commission in a rep's paycheck. The reps love to see you walk through the showroom door.

The middle-aged couple

If you are between thirty-five and fifty-five years of age, with the usual couple of kids, house, mortgage, and dog; if you both work at good jobs and drive a three- or four-year-old vehicle, then you are the dream of every sales rep in America. You've been around the block a few times, and this will probably be the fourth or fifth purchase of your lifetime. This time you've decided not to be taken in and you are going to do everything to insure the best possible deal. You've gotten "laid away" on at least one and probably two occasions. The other times you were just lucky and ended up with a rep who was a novice.

Practically every ad on TV, the radio, and in print is aimed directly at you, the middle-aged couple. These ads aimed right between your eyes will travel to your brain. Now the senses play a terrible trick on our brains. They make us see things our brain tells us we cannot afford to see. The touch of that new spotless upholstery, the feel of that quiet ride, that certain new-car smell you get, just listening to that new engine purr, and being so close to driving it off the showroom floor that you can taste it are just a few emotions that advertising pros reach and evoke when they try to pull you out of that easy chair and entice you to drop by a showroom.

You people are the backbone of the American buying public. For this reason, a large portion of this book covers the tactics that have been developed specifically to sell your age group vehicles. Please be aware of this and pay special attention. You get the most respect and consideration, the best overall treatment because you are in the best position to make that purchase now.

With this in mind, never walk into a dealership tired, mad, or upset with kids, parents, or anyone else who will distract you from the business at hand. Never go to dealerships after work or when you are hungry. Your body will urge you to act quicker than you should. Did you ever go to Las Vegas or watch people gambling? If the house is losing they bring in a fresh dealer, while the player must remain there until he loses or has sense enough to leave. When you make a vehicle purchase, you will see several fresh new faces, all of whom are trying to entice you into spending money. So be alert and don't become distracted.

The elderly

An elderly couple is another dream come true for the salesperson. Older purchasers will not usually shop for the best deal because, in many cases, they have done business with one dealer for years. They may even have bought the last several vehicles from one rep. In order to consummate the transaction rapidly, they continue to allow that person to handle their purchases, which is not a good idea. Buyers tend to place too much trust in people with whom they are used to doing business. It pays to do some comparison shopping before you make another decision. You might get a better deal somewhere else and, after all, you will deal with the service people far more often than the salesman. Even if you do buy elsewhere, you can always bring it back for servicing to the people you know best. Give it a try. Shop around to see if your rep is continuing to give you the best deal in town.

Let's have some fun

I have tried to give you some insight as to what the reps think of you and how they may treat you, as well as what they think about your buying ability. Up to now, it appears that the rep is way ahead of all buyers, but enter now several groups of buyers that drive reps absolutely crazy.

The high roller

This buyer simply walks into the car agency as if he owns it, and takes over. The salespeople are intimidated by this person's air of success and are fearful when the "roller" starts barking out commands. The heart of a sale lies in control and in knowing exactly where to take your customer. There is no controlling the high roller because he is just too strong-minded, which is why he's a success to begin with. Reps hate to see them because it's do the deal their way or else. The roller must have a rep who will ooh and ahh over his importance; only then will a sale be made. Most reps do not get excited about anyone other than themselves. To coin a phrase, "All reps are legends in their own minds."

The legal pad

This buyer enters clutching his notebook, and every rep in the place will exit the building in search of a place to hide. The legal-pad buyer is a person who wants to buy but only after extensive research to determine the best possible car for the dollar expenditure. He or she won't be buying for at least a week and maybe longer, so the rep knows ahead of time he cannot make a sale today and tries to avoid this customer like the plague. If you want the freedom to walk around a dealership "hassle-free," then carry a big yellow pad with you. You won't see a rep come close to you. They do not like giving you two hours of information and advice for free.

The pipe smoker

Everything I said about the legal pad buyer goes for the pipe smoker, plus one major attraction. This buyer wants all the information possible, then goes home to discuss it with anyone who will listen. The "thinker" will be as foxy as a chess player with the face of a poker player. The rep will be frustrated because he will be unable to tell how well his efforts are going. But, remember, Mr. Pipe Smoker, you are still dealing with a wolf dressed in fox's clothing, so don't get too cute. A seasoned rep might just call your bluff.

The businessman

This type of buyer usually exhibits many of the qualities of the high roller but lacks the latter's style, flair, and showmanship. The businessman buyer is in a hurry and can only allow a minute to discuss the deal, and only wants a bid. He tells the rep that he is obtaining bids from several other dealers and will purchase from the lowest bidder. This works once in a while, but it's likely that the rep will have friends at some of the other agencies where the businessman is planning to get bids. A simple call alerting his friend to be on the lookout for this customer will allow the pro at the other store to have fun as well. Now a slightly higher similar bid is given and our buyer will feel that since the bids are close, it must be a fair price. So, whichever dealer he ends up at makes no difference because the reps just split the commission. Not a bad day's work, and another sharp customer just got shot down in flames by a pro.

The perfect buyer (from the rep's point of view)

A family of four pulls up in a five-year-old vehicle with the kids shouting, "Can we buy this one, mommy—can we, can we?" It's the weekend and the man has the newspaper ads tucked neatly under his arm as he leaves his vehicle.

All the parties needed to make a decision are present, and the trade car has been cleaned out. A real dream, a fat commission, a big ripe tomato is there waiting to be plucked. No resistance, no shopping, no price comparison, no second baseman, no chance of getting any help, and you have to live with what is about to happen to you for only the next four or five years.

The worst possible buyer (from the rep's point of view)

Combine the strategy of the pipe smoker, the thoroughness of the legal pad, the wisdom of the elderly, the intimidation of the high roller, the ice-water veins of the businessman, the power of a woman, and the strength of the young and middle-aged buyers, and you would have a real monster on your hands if you were a car salesman. By the time you finish reading this book, you will be that monster.

Being Mentally Prepared
to Meet the Enemy

The best advice you can get

If I can teach you only one thing, it is to stick to your guns.
Once you've made up your mind to buy, do it. Once you've
decided upon the monthly payment you think you can afford, stick to it and don't go over by more than 10 percent.
Once you've decided what you believe your trade is worth,
go after that price with gusto. Even if you must advertise
it in the local paper, do it; it will be worth your small
investment in time and money. Once you've decided on the
make and model that will meet your personal needs, stick
to it. Don't be talked into another model that you know
nothing about or that is more expensive.

The biggest mistake customers make happens when
they come to buy one specific model only to find that they
cannot get the right color or perhaps the exact engine size
they requested. A sales pro can easily take advantage of
such a disappointed buyer. Customers, once they finally
decide to buy, become extremely anxious and end up want-
ing the car immediately. When they learn that they can't
get what they want, it only makes them want it even
more. Sales reps occasionally try to switch you from one
vehicle to another in order to confuse you. The buyer thus

ends up with a multitude of price, option, and payment quotes floating around in his head, none of which makes any sense at all. But, rest assured, the rep knows exactly what he has said and will rely on the fact that human nature dictates that because we hate to look stupid, we therefore won't ask questions and will try (and fail) to remember what we've been told. Was the cheaper car more per month because the term is shorter or was the more expensive vehicle cheaper each month due to a longer period to finance it? These questions are easily turned inside out by a rep who likes to play with words.

Write it down!

In order to begin our get-tough strategy, we must first agree on some ground rules. If you are going to be mentally prepared, you've got to be ready to plant some seeds in the mind of your sales rep. As soon as the "breaking the ice" portion of the sales pitch is completed, your rep will begin to take you down a road that will lead to a sale. If he says anything worthy of jotting down for later reference, do it. If you get used to writing down the important facts, you will instantly do two things. You will force your rep to be totally honest and candid with you, and if you do not purchase anything during that visit, you'll be able to refer to your notes should you return later. Even if you go to another store with the same line of cars, once the salesperson at the other agency sees that you've been doing some shopping he will only sweeten the deal. If the new rep quotes you some figures, you can then look at your notes and say, "You're going to have to do a lot better than that if you want to earn my business." Even if the notes contain no actual prices or payment figures, you'll get the rep's attention if you utter that sentence. Write it down, and start being the intimidator instead of the intimidated, right away.

Gee, I think I'll buy a car today

You don't wake up one day and say to your spouse that you are going car hunting today. I hope that your decision was a carefully planned one. If that is not a safe assumption, stop and think about your last vehicle purchase. What prompted you to go out and spend thousands of dollars? Did your neighbor or friends make a purchase? Did some advertising get you, or were you attracted by those super-low interest rates offered by the factory or by an individual dealer? Confess—did you really *have* to make that purchase or did you simply want to own a new vehicle?

As I said earlier, it is extremely important never to think that you might buy a car if the price is right! "The Price Is Right" is a terrific television game show, but you're not on TV and this is no game we're playing. Unless you take buying a car seriously, you'll end up paying several thousand dollars more than you should. Never walk into a dealership merely to look. People decide to buy for a variety of reasons; your reasons should all be good ones.

What am I trying to accomplish?

What is my purpose in making that purchase? What will I gain? Will it be a better car, will it be bigger, will it give me more performance, will the gas mileage increase? Will my insurance go up? Will my payments increase? How large a down payment will I have to produce? Could I fix my current car? What repairs would it need and how much would they cost? If I did repair my car, would its value go up? These questions along with many others should be answered before you ever venture into a showroom. On the following pages you will find several checklists that will help you determine several factors. First, you will decide whether your present vehicle can be fixed or painted to give it a new lease on life. Second, a three-part checklist will help you build a new vehicle and more important, let you begin to shop around and compare prices. Third, a personal financial form will let you see if you can afford a new vehicle.

Chart your course, your way!

The checklists in this book are designed with one purpose in mind: to make it easy for you to calculate which way is best for you. Remember our purpose: If we are to become mentally prepared to meet the enemy, then we must know some important things about ourselves even before we begin our search for a new vehicle. If, after completing the first checklist, you have decided that repairing your vehicle or adding a piece of equipment along with a new vinyl roof is not going to satisfy your needs or desires, and that you therefore are going for a new one, bravo! You've made your first decision, and you've done so through reasoning and calculating. You can now take that next important step in our program.

Part I of building your new vehicle sheet will allow you to decide which car you desire most. It will also permit you to list the features and options that you cannot live without. This information can be obtained just by dropping by a dealership for no more than ten seconds to pick up a brochure. Then, after you know the equipment you want, you or your spouse or even a friend can place a call

Are Repairs or Options What I Really Need?

HOW MUCH WILL THEY COST?

PART 1
Present Vehicle Information

Year_____Make_____Model_____Engine_____

Major Equipment Already on Car		Desired Equipment and Approximate Cost	
_____	_____	_____	$_____
_____	_____	_____	$_____
_____	_____	_____	$_____
_____	_____	_____	$_____

Total cost of desired equipment $_____
How much does value of car increase by
the addition of these new options? $_____

PART 2
Mechanical Repairs Needed

_____	$_____
_____	$_____
_____	$_____
_____	$_____
_____	$_____
Total	$_____

PART 3
Cosmetic Repairs Needed

_____	$_____
_____	$_____
_____	$_____
_____	$_____
Total	$_____

Total Part 1	$_____
Part 2	$_____
Part 3	$_____
Grand Total	$_____

Summary: If I decided to make the repairs listed, would my needs and goals be met?

Building My New Vehicle

PART I

FEATURES AND PRICES

Year_____Make_____Model_____
Body Style_____Engine Size_____Horsepower_____
Color Choices: 1st_____2nd_____3rd_____
Upholstery Fabric (check one): Cloth__Velour__Vinyl__Leather__
Upholstery Colors: 1st_____2nd_____

Standard Features Already on Car

_____ _____ _____
_____ _____ _____
_____ _____ _____
_____ _____ _____
_____ _____ _____

Desired Options or Special Features

_____ _____ _____
_____ _____ _____
_____ _____ _____

Prices I Received over the Telephone or Through My Own Research

1) Base price $_____   NOTES AND
2) Total of all options $_____   COMMENTS
3) Freight fee $_____
4) **Total** $_____
5) Plus local sales tax $_____
6) License fee $_____
7) Other (A) $_____
8) Other (B) $_____
9) **Total price delivered** $_____
   to you
10) Less trade allowance   −$_____
11) Less cash down payment   −$_____

12) **Net Total**   = _____   Amount to
                                                  finance at bank

PART 2

Specific Equipment and Its Approximate Cost

ON THIS SHEET LIST OPTIONAL EQUIPMENT PRICES TO PERMIT
YOU TO ADJUST MONTHLY PAYMENTS OR PRICE OF VEHICLE TO
FIT YOUR BUDGET

Option	Approximate Cost	Actual Cost
1) _____	$_____	$_____
2) _____	_____	_____
3) _____	_____	_____
4) _____	_____	_____
5) _____	_____	_____
6) _____	_____	_____
7) _____	_____	_____
8) _____	_____	_____
9) _____	_____	_____
10) _____	_____	_____
11) _____	_____	_____
12) _____	_____	_____
13) _____	_____	_____
14) _____	_____	_____
15) _____	_____	_____
Totals	$_____	$_____

NOTES

PART 3

Options or Services I Can Get Outside the Dealership and Pay for Separately

THIS LIST COMPARES THE PRICE CHARGED BY THE DEALERSHIP AND ELSEWHERE

Services	Dealer Price	Comparison Price
1) Paint sealant package	$_____	$_____
2) Undercoating	_____	_____
3) Fabric protection	_____	_____
4) Body side molding	_____	_____
5) Accent stripes	_____	_____
6) Vinyl roof	_____	_____
7) Electric sun roof	_____	_____
8) Manual sun roof	_____	_____
9) Special tires	_____	_____
10) Special wheels	_____	_____
11) Special equipment for truck	_____	_____
A)_____	_____	_____
B)_____	_____	_____
12) Sheepskin covers	_____	_____
13) Mud flaps or guards	_____	_____
14) Real spare tire	_____	_____
15) Special radio	_____	_____
16) Other_____	_____	_____
Totals	$_____	$_____

NOTE: If any of these services is performed outside the dealership, how will I pay for it? How much of my cash down payment could I use on this list and still have my payments remain the same?

Personal Financial Statement

Monthly Expenses

Rent or mortgage	$_____
Gas	_____
Electricity	_____
Water, sewage	_____
Garbage pick-up	_____
Medical (all)	_____
Savings	_____
School tuition	_____
Insurance (car, boat)	_____
Insurance (home, life, health, medical)	_____
Telephone	_____
_____	_____
_____	_____
_____	_____
Car payment(s) (now)	_____
2nd mtge payment	_____
Personal credit line	_____
Charge accounts	_____
_____	_____
_____	_____
_____	_____
_____	_____
_____	_____
Other loan payments	_____
Food (average)	_____
Clothing	_____
Entertainment	_____
Misc._____	_____
Misc._____	_____
Total monthly bills	$_____

Monthly Income

My take-home pay	$_____
Spouse take-home pay	_____
Other take-home pay (family or boarder)	_____
Part-time job	_____
Interest income	_____
Stock dividends	_____
Investment income	_____
Property income	_____
Rental income	_____
Side business	_____
Service performed	_____
Other income	_____
Other income	_____
Total monthly income	$_____

The real, real bottom line

Total monthly income	$_____
Total monthly outgo	− $_____
Left after bills	= $_____

Can I really afford a new car?

Yes_____ No_____

to the car agency and ask for the sales manager. It may take a phone call or two to get through to him (as a former sales manager I used to get 150–200 different calls per day) but, when you do, simply inform him that you might be in the market for a vehicle soon and would he be good enough to give you some help on prices of the different models and equipment. Doing this will cause two things to happen. First, the sales manager won't usually have the time to chat about prices so he will turn you over to either an assistant or a sales rep; second, the person who does end up giving you the prices will do so precisely and quickly because the manager has directed him to do so. He will think that you are a VIP and will gladly give you the information you need. When you are finished, just say that you will be in touch, thank him for his time, and hang up. There is no need for further conversation because the rep will think that you will be getting back to the manager. You will have the prices on both the model and the options.

Part 2 of the checklist asks you to estimate the price of a particular option. For fun, try guessing to see if you can come close. You might get sticker shock before you even get to the dealership.

You're gaining valuable knowledge

Because you will be in the privacy and comfort of your own home, I think that you will find this rather enjoyable. It really is fun to buy a car or truck, at least until you have to confront a hungry sales rep. And while doing these little exercises, you'll become knowledgeable about the vehicle you wish to purchase. You will become familiar with the product, its equipment, its prices, and even the freight charges. You'll know whether or not you can get some of the options or services installed or performed outside the agency, how much they will cost, and how much you might save. You will, at your own pace, become as familiar with the car you intend to buy as your sales rep. Imagine how confident you will feel when you do end up doing battle with your sales rep. You will know where you stand financially and can adjust the equipment and options to fit your budget, all without divulging any personal information to a stranger. You will be in control of the entire situation from the outset. Now, doesn't that put you in a much better position than the last time you tried to make a purchase?

Let's go all the way

I guess you think you're now ready to make a reasonable decision and chart your course. Not yet! I want you to be as familiar with this deal as possible. It is my intention to have you feel as if you've been to the dealership before you go. Consequently, there are three more important items that you must address before you leave home: your payments, your insurance rates, and the worth of your trade-in. The next checklists will assist you in finding out the answers to these important questions. But they will require you to do some more legwork. But it's worth it.

My Monthly Payment Calculations

HOW TO CALCULATE THE AMOUNT TO FINANCE

Price of vehicle	$_____
+ sales tax	$_____
+ license fees	$_____
+ dealer doc fees	$_____
+ any other fee	$_____
= **total**	$_____
− trade allowance	$_____
− cash down	$_____
= **balance**	$_____

Bank Quotations Over the Phone

Call three banks for rates and payment quotes. Get a straight payment quote with no credit insurance included!

Name of bank_____   Length of term_____
Location_____   Interest Rate_____
Phone number_____   Required down payment_____
Banker's name_____   Monthly payment $_____

Name of bank_____   Length of term_____
Location_____   Interest rate_____
Phone number_____   Required down payment_____
Banker's name_____   Monthly payment $_____

Name of bank_____   Length of term_____
Location_____   Interest rate_____
Phone number_____   Required down payment_____
Banker's name_____   Monthly payment $_____

Obtain these quotes even if you plan to take advantage of a special dealer/factory finance program. You will have peace of mind knowing exactly how much you will be paying each month.

Insurance Quotes and/or Bids

NEW VEHICLE INFORMATION YOU'LL NEED TO GET A QUOTE

Vehicle year_____   Engine size_____
Vehicle make_____   Horsepower_____
Model_____   Value_____
Type_____   Other_____

AGENT INFORMATION

Carrier_____   Agent_____
Location_____   Phone_____

LIMITS AND COVERAGES

_____Deductible comprehensive @ $_____
_____Deductible collision @ $_____
_____Fire, theft, towing @ $_____
_____Other @ $_____
_____Property damage @ $_____
_____Uninsured motorist fund @ $_____
_____Limits of liability @ $_____
                 Total $_____

Get a Second Opinion

SECOND OPINION

Carrier_____   Agent_____
Location_____   Phone_____

LIMITS AND COVERAGES

_____Deductible comprehensive @ $_____
_____Deductible collision @ $_____
_____Fire, theft, towing @ $_____
_____Other @ $_____
_____Property damage @ $_____
_____Uninsured motorist fund @ $_____
_____Limits of liability @ $_____
                 Total $_____

PART 1

Evaluating My Trade Vehicle:

Year_____   Present Mileage_____

Make_____   Body Type_____

Model_____   Engine Size_____

EQUIPMENT

_____	_____	_____
_____	_____	_____
_____	_____	_____
_____	_____	_____

INSTRUCTIONS FOR DETERMINING VALUE

1) Plan to spend one full hour in the middle of the week.

2) Go to your banker first. It should be the same person from whom you obtained payment quotes.

3) Ask the banker to review with you his used-car guide (blue book, red book, NADA book, black book, Kelly guide).

4) Determine the wholesale value and retail value of your vehicle with the banker. (Use part 2 of this sheet.)

5) Do not concern yourself with any reconditioning costs or repairs.

6) Don't forget to deduct for any excess mileage on your vehicle.

7) With the figures from your banker in hand, go get three independent bids from three automobile dealers. Go to one used-car dealer and two new-car dealers.

8) Tell the managers that you would like to sell them your vehicle and ask to be given a buy bid right there on the spot. A buy bid is the amount the dealer would pay you in cash for your car at that very moment. It is what the agency really believes the vehicle is worth.

9) If they will not give you a buy figure, then ask them what it might be worth on the market. Try to get some estimate from them. If you can't, do not waste your time; go to another dealer.

10) This entire process should be completed within one hour. After you finish, sit down and compare what the banker figured with what the dealers calculated your vehicle was worth. **Now, try to figure how much you would have to spend on your vehicle to put it in tip-top shape.** (Use the figures from the first checklist to help you.) Once you determine the reconditioning cost, deduct that figure from the banker's total (wholesale) figure and you should be close to the dealer amount.

NOTE: Dealers will give you wholesale amounts or bids. Should you decide to attempt to retail your vehicle, add about fifteen hundred dollars to the wholesale amounts and you should then have a good starting figure or asking price.

PART 2

Evaluating My Trade Vehicle: at the Bank

Base book wholesale	$_____	Retail base	$_____
Excess mileage, deduct	_____	Mileage, deduct	_____
Net wholesale amount	$_____	Net retail	$_____

WHOLESALE EQUIPMENT ADDS

RETAIL EQUIP-
MENT ADDS

Description	Amount Added	Retail Amount Added
_____	$_____	$_____
_____	_____	_____
_____	_____	_____
_____	_____	_____
_____	_____	_____
_____	_____	_____
_____	_____	_____
_____	_____	_____
_____	_____	_____
_____	_____	_____
_____	_____	_____
_____	_____	_____
_____	_____	_____
_____	_____	_____
Total both columns	$_____	$_____
+ Net base amount	_____	_____
= Final net amount	$_____	$_____

Name of bank_____
Name of banker_____

USED-CAR BUY BIDS

First dealer _____Manager's name _____
First dealer bid $_____Good till _____
Second dealer _____Manager's name _____
Second dealer bid $_____Good till _____
Third dealer _____Manager's name _____
Third dealer bid $_____Good till _____

Now compare your findings.

Easier than you thought

Now that wasn't very difficult, was it? Things always look harder than they actually are. I had you do it this way for several reasons. First, you now have a bit more experience in talking to bankers and automobile department managers. Second, you know the real bottom line on your trade vehicle and can sensibly decide whether to trade or sell. Third, you will know how much you can finance in order that the payment which you were quoted will remain the same. In addition, if your banker wanted your business, he probably offered a great deal of "free" information and advice regarding your upcoming purchase.

Nearly ready to get serious

We are now almost ready to meet the enemy. We know the model we wish to purchase and have a good idea of its total cost. We know the sales tax and license fees and whether the insurance rates will increase. We also have a good idea of what our trade vehicle is worth and what the monthly payments should be, and we have studied the brochures from the dealership on the car or truck we want. We are almost ready to go into battle.

We must now do what all great generals do before a great battle; namely, scouting and reconnaissance. We must find out which dealers are having big sales and special promotions, which dealer or manufacturer is doing the most television and/or newspaper advertising. You must put yourself in touch with the car marketplace. Start reading those ads.

Wanna buy a lawn mower?

Think about this: If you were not in the market for a lawn mower, then all the advertising in the world could not attract your attention. If a fancy TV ad offered the mowers at 50 percent off, you would never even hear the message because you would be at the refrigerator during the commercial. But if you did need a new mower and were considering buying one soon, that ad would get your undivided attention.

The same thing applies to the auto industry. If you watch TV or listen to the radio enough, you might think that all you hear are car and truck ads. Get this deal here and get the deal of a lifetime now is all you ever see and hear anymore. That's because each week a new set of buyers is ready to attack the car agencies of America. The buyers who bought or tried to buy last week are ancient history. This week's buyers are now the targets. That's why dealers seem to have a perpetual sale. Some dealers have fifty-two clearance sales a year, one each week, but we all know that a sale is not always a bargain. It is you, the consumer, who must make a bargain happen by being in the right place at the right time. But that is luck, you say. I believe in making your own luck.

Timing is of the essence

How can you figure out how to be in the right place at the right time? It's easy. When I was a sales manager, part of my responsibility was to establish dollar targets for the new car sales department for the next month. Occasionally I bit off more than I could chew. My projections were often too high, and I would find myself accepting just about any deal (sometimes losing money on certain vehicles) when the end of the month rolled around. I always wondered if my customers ever knew how lucky they were to have come in at the end of the month when I was hungry to make my target. Most sales managers work on a bonus system; if they meet or exceed the projected sales figures, they are rewarded handsomely. So, take your time, read the newspapers, and wait until the end of the month to make that purchase.

If you are smart, you will first go to the dealership as they're closing on a Sunday to find the vehicle that best meets your needs. You can accomplish so much when you are not bothered by a hungry sales rep. Since you've done your preliminary research, all you need now is the stock number of the car that comes closest to fitting your needs. Then, when you do go during regular hours, you can get a test drive in that particular model, without having to go through any hassle. You will be in control of your deal, and you must get used to having the dealer and his staff doing things your way.

The Mind Game War Begins

What is a "mind game"?

Let's define the term *mind game* as it pertains to the automobile business. Webster's dictionary defines *game* as "a contest of strength, skill or chance, for sport or for a stake, a scheme or plan." We all know what *mind* means; therefore, *mind game* might be a contest that tests the strength of the mind for a certain stake. If so, for a game to exist, there must be something at stake.

What is important here is the attitude that we were taught as children: that it's not whether you win or lose, it's how you play the game. A fine statement, and never more true than in the car business. This so-called mind game pits you against a professional. Buying a car has become a game for the pro and a nightmare for most customers. The dealers are set up to win the game. It is their plan to be as profitable as possible. These people who call themselves "dealers" have very appropriately and correctly named themselves. They are in business to win, to be number one or die trying to reach that goal. But, you ask, how can an ordinary citizen hope to compete against such odds? Its like trying to fight city hall. You can fight but can you ever win? I say you can and will as long as you're no gambler. But, you say, you never gamble—oh, maybe ten bucks on a football game or on the World Series, but never anything greater than that.

Not true. Every time you come up against a professional automobile salesman, you are gambling, and with the potential of losing thousands. Webster's dictionary defines *gambler* as "one who plays games of chance." You might as well go to Las Vegas or Atlantic City and have some real fun. There, at least, you'll feel as though you're getting your money's worth in entertainment. A vehicle costs so much that there is no reason to pay more than you have to. By paying more for the car, you get no more for your money.

Breaking it down

It is necessary to distinguish two different kinds of these "mind game" wars. We will start at the beginning. For ages, dealers have collectively met to discuss how to be more profitable while assuming no more risk. Thus, in a metropolitan area of one million people, it is possible to forecast, within a few percentage points, the number of vehicles each manufacturer should sell in any given model year. With that projection in hand, dealers try to insure that these targets are met or even surpassed. If a dealer is going to get one hundred potential buyers in his showroom during a business week, and his sales staff has a closing ratio of 25 percent, then it doesn't take much to see that the dealer will sell about twenty-five vehicles during that week. But what happened to the other seventy-five, the potential buyers who didn't buy? They either went to another dealership or put off any purchase. Maybe some found the vehicles too expensive, maybe others could not find the right color. Whatever the reason, seventy-five buyers walked out without making a purchase. Now some would say that if this dealer wants to increase business, he must first attract more people to his agency. But that usually means spending more money to advertise. However, what if he could sell another twenty-five cars to the seventy-five people who left without buying? Then the dealer would have a 50 percent closing ratio without spending another dime to get the increased business and revenue. The question then becomes: How does he increase closing averages by twenty-five points? The answer is to develop a system, use it, and stick to it.

System selling

The great advantage of "system selling" is that it makes far greater use of the existing customers than ever before. A system insures not only that customers are greeted in a certain manner, but that they will not be allowed out the door unless a manager permits it. In a few cases customers become extremely angry and end up storming out of the showroom in disgust once they realize what is happening.

Here's how it works. A system consists of what's called a "liner" or "greeter," followed by a long line of closers and grinders. The sole job of the liner is to set you up to buy a vehicle. This person, usually a young, clean-cut, all-American type with red cheeks and pearly teeth, will take you to the car or truck of your dreams; once you begin to inquire as to the price, you are ushered into a closing booth where you undergo a series of systematic approaches that, professionals always say, will lead to a sale at least 50 percent of the time.

The road to a sale (or the steps to success)

Each system incorporates certain proven steps. They are as follows:

1. Greet the customer
2. Zero customer in on one vehicle
3. Thorough product presentation
4. Evaluate customer
5. Thorough vehicle demonstration
6. Present product video tapes
7. Ask for sale or trial close
8. Overcome objections
9. Turn to closer
10. Closer turns to second closer
11. Customer is continued to be worked until he buys or dies
12. Once sale is closed, follow-up system is started by asking for referrals

Every dealer has some sort of system, nearly all of which are some variation of the standard TO (turnover) system. Under this system, a dealer can fine-tune various presentations and closes to improve areas of weakness in the sales pitch. Some systems are so thorough they include exact dialogue on everything from the greeting to the close and how hard or soft you should be on your prospect. The best system conceals from the buyer any idea that it even exists.

You can compare an accomplished sales professional to an actor. One never thinks of an actor staying up late to study his lines, but of course he does. The same applies to professional sales reps. They get so much practice on customers that after only a few weeks the pitch sounds honest and genuine and loaded with integrity, which is how it's supposed to sound.

I'll bet this is just what you're looking for, sir

Under a good system, reps are trained to get you, the buyer, to answer as many questions as possible. Questions like this: "Do you want a two-door or four-door? A four-cylinder, a six-cylinder, or even an eight? What is your favorite color? Are you looking for a big car or little car? A four-wheel-drive or two-wheel-drive pickup? Where did you finance your last vehicle? How much do you owe on your trade? When do you intend to buy? Have you been shopping long? The list is endless. These are all reasonable questions that inform the reps as to your intentions. Notice also the word "NO" cannot be used to answer these questions. Once the rep obtains the necessary answers, you will be led down a smooth route that will ultimately lead to your demise.

Prequalifying customers

Do you remember, earlier in the book, how a rep could determine no fewer than eight different things from the answers to a few brief questions? How much do you think he will be able to tell from a two-hour conversation? If a professional automobile sales rep is still with you after two hours, it's only because you gave him the correct answers during the qualifying period. Each question, regardless of its nature, gives a pro more reason either to continue the sale or to drop you. Tell this veteran that you won't be purchasing for a month or two and hear how his voice drops a note or two. Then watch him figure out a way to "lot-drop" you gently and move on to another suspect.

By answering the questions for your rep, you'll just be setting yourself up for problems down the road. The less information you offer, the harder it will be for the pro to figure you out. It will be difficult for him to judge what type of buyer you are. If asked a question other than one pertaining to the type of vehicle you are interested in, simply reply "no" or "what difference could it possibly make." You can even get cute if you like as long as you do not give any indication of your present intentions or your past actions. It's none of their business. You never know: you name the dealership where you purchased last and mention the name of the rep who sold you, and a veteran pro might know him. They might even be best of friends. A quick phone call to your old salesperson could end up being the last nail in your coffin. Keep your mouth closed and your ears open! Let the rep do all the talking. Ask a few technical questions of your own regarding the vehicle to see if this professional really knows the product. Then decide whether he is good enough to earn the right to sell you a new vehicle. This is a great way to get control of the situation and the sale. Take charge and be strong because you are the person who is going to be signing your name to a finance contract or writing a check for thousands of dollars.

The product presentation

The next step in the controlled system will be a thorough product presentation. If you did your homework, you should know almost everything about the vehicle, so this will serve as a refresher course. You'll get to see at firsthand how some of the options work and you can ask about onboard computer systems. Never allow your sales rep to dodge your questions about any part of the car. For example, if you plan to tow a boat or trailer, you will want to know about factory-recommended towing capacities, the best transmissions and engines, and the towing packages available, as well as any other aspects that could affect the car's operation and even the warranty. Vehicles in stock on dealer lots hardly ever include special towing equipment; however, a rep may imply that the vehicle will do the job even without those heavy-duty shocks. So, if you ask a question, get an answer. Don't let the rep skip over anything. If you have been listening so far, you'll have your legal pad in hand, and when you ask a question that either doesn't get an answer or gets an answer that you don't like, simply jot it down and ask it again a few minutes later. If your rep sees that you are not going to allow him to get away with anything, he'll get his act together fast. He'll know that you are no easy mark. A cautious rep will pass along the fact that you're a sharp, tough customer to his superiors, which will be taken into consideration when you begin your price negotiations. You must establish that you're not a pushover. Simply turn things around and put your sales rep and the entire dealership to the test. Do your own qualifying and make certain it's you who fires the first shot instead of your opponent. Get tough. You can do it!

The demo ride

Once your desire to take this beautiful brand-new vehicle on a test drive becomes so strong you can taste it, the rep may allow you to drive the car. I said *may* allow. Quite often reps see that you are eager to see how it handles, and they will purposely make you wait and sometimes make you ask several times to drive the vehicle. After all, the more emotional you become for the product, the more you will end up paying.

Once you do get behind the wheel, you will generally go down a planned route. This course will include turns, potholes, and maybe a hill or two so that you get a complete picture of the performance and feel of your new vehicle. As you drive, a good rep will take the occasion to plant a seed in your mind, something like, "Well, Mr. Smith, how does it feel? Just think what your neighbors are going to say when you pull up in your driveway in this beauty. You'll be the envy of the entire neighborhood. Did you tell anyone that you were going to buy a new car today? I'll bet you will have to fight Mrs. Smith for the keys when you get home. By the way, who will be driving it home today?" These hints, even if you deny or counter them, cause you to see yourself drive up to your house as all the neighbors peek out of their windows marveling at your new car. The old saying, a picture is worth a thousand words, was never more appropriate. In fact, if you slip up and say in a joking manner that you'll be the one who will drive home today in the new car, then you have already purchased the car in your mind and the rep has actually closed the sale. That is what I mean by a "mind game."

Many times during the sales pitch and demo ride a rep will make such suggestions in order to keep your enthusiasm at the highest level. After all, you really would like to own this vehicle, but your mind prevents you from taking the final leap too quickly. Unless all the questions are answered and you are able to decide that the purchase is a sound move, you will end up in conflict in your own mind. If, however, you know exactly what a professional may do, then you must get a great deal on the vehicle of your dreams. So if your rep tries to suggest a picture of you driving up to your house, turn it around on him. Ask the rep if he will enjoy spending the commission from your sale, provided he has earned the right to sell you. Make sure he is aware that he has not yet earned your business. This provocative statement will keep the rep off balance and force him to do a better job of selling. Again, you will keep control of the sale in your hands.

A hard move to counter

At the end of the test drive reps will sometimes ask to drive the new vehicle back themselves so they can show you something of importance, or else to let you relax in your new vehicle during the drive back to the dealership. In either case, the rep, who knows what you drove up in, will pull the new vehicle next to your old car. If you insist on driving back, the rep will have you stop where he would have parked, or he will ask you to pull the car in the "sold" line. Obviously, pulling up next to your old trade needs no explanation. If you follow directions and pull into the sold line, you admit to yourself that you have just bought a car.

The moment of silence

At the moment you turn the engine off and begin to exit from the demo ride, a horrible fact hits you. The pleasantries are over; it's time for some serious business. There is nothing more to do except to negotiate. As the rep pulls onto the dealer property he has already decided exactly how to get you from the vehicle to the closing room. Whether he says, "Come into my office so we can do some old-fashioned horse trading" or "Let's go inside and figure out how much damage we've done here today," a good rep will say it, then turn around, and start walking toward his office. This takes some concentration on his part because he is trained to assume that his customers will follow him like puppies. Consequently, he cannot look back to see whether, in fact, his customers are really trailing behind him or have gotten in their car and left. In ninety-nine out of one hundred cases the customer, in an attempt to keep from looking or feeling ridiculous, will be there on the rep's heels as they get to the closing office. It hardly ever fails. It will be one of the longest walks you'll ever take. During this quiet stroll to the office, you and your spouse, or perhaps a friend, will have no idea of what is going to happen next. You assume that you'll get down to the nitty-gritty and wonder whether you can agree on a good price. It's the not knowing what or how the rep will attempt to get your signature on the dotted line that really scares you. Will he lie to me? If he does, how will I know? I don't even know this person, how can I trust him? I really want a new car but will I get a good deal? How much should I pay? I'll just tell him that I don't feel well and leave, but he has spent two hours with me and I can't do that. Was the rep at the other store telling me the truth? These questions race through your mind at the speed of light and you quickly become insecure.

Wanna play games with a pro . . . now?

If you have not done your homework, any hope you had of winning the game has all but collapsed right here, at the moment when you entered the office to enter into negotiations. Up to now, most dealerships—"system" sellers or not—use the same selling techniques listed above. However, now is when dealerships separate the men from the boys. Agencies operating under rigid systems will attack you immediately. They will never beat around the bush; on the contrary, they go right after your wallet. It has been fun looking at all the vehicles and picking out a car or truck. Now it's time to pay. It's time to lay out the cash, put your John Hancock on the dotted line, and live for the next four or five years with what you do in the next thirty minutes. Are you prepared to make a decision that you might regret each time you drive this mistake down the street? Did you reveal too much to your sales rep? You'd better be sure of what you're doing or else pay thousands more than necessary. I do not know which is worse, paying too much or paying for something that you didn't really want to begin with. Do your homework and get the facts straight before you enter a closing booth. The decision then is yours as to whether you win or lose.

You may qualify for frequent flier discounts

Fasten your seat belt and prepare for the roller-coaster ride of your life. In the next thirty to sixty minutes a strong sales rep and a good manager will take you up and down so many times that you'll qualify for frequent flier discounts. You'll be launched into orbit the first time you hear the total price. Then after you are assured that this is only the asking price (you will still be in orbit, however), the professional who does this each and every day of the year will launch you into deep space. Have a nice trip. This will occur when he informs you of the discount you'll be getting if he can talk the boss into being so generous. You'll leave the solar system when the discount is only about one-quarter of the amount you thought you could get. Don't get excited! Coolly and gracefully the rep is trying to force you to get used to a higher price. He is simply taking your temperature, feeling you out. This is the object of the exercise.

But because the rep tells you that the most you can possibly receive as a discount is a few hundred dollars, you don't have to believe him. Since we're playing mind games, let's really play and have some fun. If you want to see a grown person cry and can keep yourself under control when you are given the initial price, just do the following.

Return the favor

As soon as they attempt to insult your honor, intelligence, and integrity by giving you a ridiculous price, just get up and say, "Sir, we have nothing more to discuss," and walk out of the office and head slowly for the door. Act both indignant and insulted. You will see your startled sales rep, with egg on his face, begin an extraordinary series of apologies. To say the least, you'll have the ball on the five-yard line and it will be first and goal. Then, when you do allow him another chance to sell you, you've already laid down some important ground rules that must be met before you will continue. The rep will quickly inform his manager what has happened because under most systems the manager's desk is on or near the showroom floor, and he can plainly see a problem if it occurs, especially if you're loud and candid. The rep will ask you back in the booth and retreat to the manager's office for new instructions. It is unlikely that the rep has ever come up against someone like you. He will need a new game plan, for the old one has been destroyed. By the way, welcome back to earth. Did you wave at your sales rep as he flew by when you returned the favor and launched him into space?

How do you feel?

Now that you've traded some blows with your salesman, how do you feel? Did you ever think so much preparation went into a simple thing like buying a car? The point of this chapter is to make you aware that these mind games really do exist. At this point in your car-buying education, however, I just want you to realize the scope of what you face and the speed with which you can regain the upper hand should you have to. As we progress, I will give you plenty of firepower to use against your salesman. In Chapter 4 we discuss the various tactics and goals of the different systems so you may fully understand how effective this kind of selling can be. Furthermore, since the system is really a big mind game itself, you will be able to counteract it better when you find yourself in a similar position. These systems are designed solely to confuse and wear you out. In this example, by the time you get to the point of doing battle, you've been skirmishing for nearly two hours, but a manager has yet to come in and attempt to close you. When this happens, you can expect to be at the agency for another hour, or as long as it takes for the team to get the job done. You are just one person facing a professional system that is designed to win. Teaching you to take on the system is the reason this book is in your hands.

4

The Mind Game War
Continues

How to recognize system selling

At first it may be difficult for you to detect a system at all, and the chances of identifying which system it is are slim. That's because you must first get halfway through the system itself before you can distinguish its particular technique. At that point it may be hard for you to adjust your thoughts to those of your counterpart. Remember, until you finish the demo ride, most agencies' techniques are essentially the same. Therefore, if you can't immediately establish their game plan, don't worry. You'll soon get a feel which way the salesperson is leaning by the direction he takes you. Do not resist as the rep begins to nudge you along; permit him to take you down whichever road he pleases.

There are four main ways a system works, but in all of them the rep seeks to identify your "hot button" so that he can most effectively close the sale. There are four paths because there are four aspects of the sale, one of which will affect you most: the selling price, the trade allowance, the cash down payment and/or the amount of discount, or the amount of the monthly payments. Even if you are interested in each of them, one will predominate; an anxious buyer will usually want this question answered as soon as possible. For example, if you said several times that you wanted monthly payments of a certain amount and the rep replied each time with a statement like, "Let's pick out a vehicle first, then my manager will answer your questions regarding payments," that alerts you to the existence of a system; were there no system, the rep would attempt to close the deal immediately. If your rep was not under strict orders to go a certain route without deviating from it, then why would he go through all the aggravation of a systemized sales presentation? A real professional would seize the opportunity and close then and there. Furthermore, the more resistance you offer, once you realize the system does exist, the faster a manager will arrive on the scene. Usually the first manager to arrive in the TO system will be a team leader or shift leader. To compare this person to a second lieutenant in the army might give him a bit more credit than he deserves. Keep in mind one thing, as you continue to say "no" you will be confronted with a battery of closers who will show you through the ranks all the way up to a colonel, or general sales manager. Everyone will take his or her best shot at you in an effort to close the sale. In fact, the higher up you get, the better the deal will be. Never be afraid to talk to the powers that be at an agency.

The write-up

When you must go through a system to make a purchase, it can be tedious. The salesperson must follow directions, and the necessity for some of the steps is unclear. For example, each dealer has his own method of submitting a deal to the "desk." Either a work sheet, copy of a buyer's order, scrap paper, legal pad, or a combination will get the job done. The object is to get some sort of commitment on paper. A sharp rep may say, "Well, Mr. Smith, I know you have some figures in mind—after all, you're no dummy— so tell me what they are and I'm going to 'write up' this offer, get your signature on it, and submit it to my manager for approval." Sounds pretty straightforward and honest, correct? As a matter of fact, if you haven't done your homework and don't know how much to offer, you'll be in deep water.

The system is designed to force you to make some decisions which you may not be able to make. Should you reply to your straightforward rep that you want to pay as little as possible and that if he wants your business he should give you the best price now, before you get up and leave, you've played right into their hands. The rep will almost always respond with, "OK, sir, my dealer allows me on my own to discount this vehicle $150; therefore, I'll do it right now for you and get the rest of the paperwork started so you folks can drive home in it. How does that sound, Mr. Smith, is that fair enough?" (There you go again, heading for outer space as you think the guy has a lot of nerve offering you a lousy $150 off the sticker.)

Let's stop right here for a moment. You just told the rep that you want his best deal right now. Well, he just gave it to you. He just said that he has given you the most his dealer will allow him to give you. So why are you upset? You got what you asked for, didn't you? Now everyone in the whole world knows that it isn't enough and won't be enough. The rep knows it, the dealer knows it, you know it, the managers know it, your friend or spouse knows it, even your dog knows it. But what do you do now? The professional has just forced you to make an offer. After you respond that he is crazy, and your blood pressure has gone up dangerously, you say to the rep there's no way you will accept a measly $150 off sticker. But the customer makes that response every time. You see, the rep's object here is to insult your intelligence by offering you such a low discount that you get mad and, in anger, respond with an emphatic no. At this point, with you steaming, the rep's reply will be, "Gee, Mr. Smith, I'm sorry you're so upset. I never meant to make you angry but sir, this is all I am allowed to offer you. If you require a larger discount, just tell me how much you want, let me put it on paper, get your signature, then I'll go to my boss with your offer and try to talk him into accepting it. Now, is that fair enough?"

No matter what you say now, you're dead. Even if you repeat that you still want their best deal, you've already received it. Any additional discount will come only after you have made an offer yourself. No matter what you propose, it will be written down and you will have to sign next to it before your offer can be submitted. Incidentally, you can demand till you're blue in the face that the manager make you an offer, and you will never succeed. One of the first rules in any negotiation is that once you make a statement, never go back on it. If you were able to convince the rep to reconsider his position, and he allowed you $500 discount without going to his manager, he would lose all credibility and you, the buyer, would have scored a resounding victory. But it will never happen. Once the dealer and his staff commit to something, they will not back down. Besides, they realize that you have consumed a great deal of time and energy. Having gone this far, you will not want to go through this ordeal again at another agency. As a matter of fact, they will almost always be right.

These people are professionals. They know exactly what makes you tick and what buttons to push to obtain the response they want. It's human nature.

You're not done yet

As you see, some systems are designed to force the issue and make you submit an offer, while others just zero in on your hot button: payments, cash down or discount, trade allowance, and selling price. An efficient way for a good rep to identify the one that affects you the most is to write them down on paper. You'll be amazed at what most customers end up doing.

Let's assume you are interested in purchasing a vehicle with a sticker price of $10,955.92, and you have indicated to your rep that your payments cannot exceed $230 per month. In addition, you feel that your trade vehicle is worth $2500, which is why you won't be coming up with a cash down payment. Moreover, at the last car store you visited, the rep told you that you could get at least $1000 in discount off the sticker price of a similar vehicle. You've been with your rep for nearly two hours, and you have said that you will not purchase today and, in fact, are not going to buy for a couple of weeks.

Does this sound like the customer has a good grip on the situation? He is frank and sure of himself, and it appears as if he has done his homework and knows exactly what he can afford as well as how much he is willing to pay. The rep has not disputed any of the customer's demands. As a professional, the rep first must review this potential deal to insure that the figures are correct. After checking the numbers, which are accurate, the rep asks for the buyer's signature and the assurance that the customer will buy if these demands are met. Who wouldn't? After all, these are your own figures.

The rep returns a few minutes later from the manager with the following counter-offer.

Customer Work Sheet

Name_____   Date_____

Address_____   Phone_____

WANTS TO PURCHASE THE FOLLOWING

Year_____Make_____Model_____

YOUR SELLING PRICE	YOUR TRADE AMOUNT
$_____10,480.92_____	$_____1300_____

YOUR MONTHLY PAYMENTS	YOUR DISCOUNT AMOUNT
$_275.89 × 48 @ 9.9% APR_ with $1500 cash down payment	$_____475_____

You must understand one fact before we go on. Each of these items contains the largest possible profit or, in other words, the worst possible terms for the buyer. Notice the small discount, the large down payment, the long term of the payments, the high selling price, the poor trade allowance, and the high monthly payment. In fact, nothing about this deal even remotely resembles the deal with which the sales rep left. Again, it's time to put on your flight suit and prepare for earth orbit. Good-bye!!

You may ask, How can they have the nerve to make such an offer? They must be out of their minds. On the contrary, they have just made a brilliant move. You are in shock, and your mind is racing in order to comprehend what has happened. Doubt begins to take over. You not only begin to doubt what you are doing but your own calculations as well. The first thing you ask yourself is how could you be so far off on *all* the items. You didn't even come close to getting even one right. With such thoughts, all you can think of is compromise. You came here to buy a car today and you really did your homework; at least you thought you did. You shopped around but you now conclude that the other salespeople were just telling you what you wanted to hear instead of the truth.

Before, it was all going your way, but now you tell yourself that if only you can get the dealer to compromise just a little, you will gladly purchase and end this nightmare. Is it the monthly payments or the trade allowance that's most important? Or perhaps the discount—that's not enough. I've got to come up with $1500 cash and I don't have that much in my bank account. Maybe I can get them to reduce the payments by going for sixty months instead of forty-eight. All this races through the buyer's mind while the rep is calmly sitting, smiling, and not uttering a sound. He is just waiting, as he is trained to do, for your response. Then he will attack you with the most devastating psychological devices he can muster. Everything he will propose will sound fair and reasonable. If you said, "Look, you're not giving me enough for my trade vehicle; I can't accept that figure," the rep would remind you that you can always sell the trade privately and remove it from the deal. But, you respond, that may take days or weeks. "Well, what if I go back to my boss and see if he can get you some additional money from the used-car department for your trade?" the rep says. "What will it take for me to get an order for you to purchase today?" You reply, "If you can get me $2000 for my car and lower those payments to about $230 per month, I'll buy right now." (You think that you were cool to slip those monthly payments in there, and you know they must have some room to move on your trade. You're not as dumb as they think you are.)

Guess what? You've just committed financial suicide. Here's why: Nine times out of ten the trade vehicle would have been appraised for much higher than the offer on the work sheet. The work sheet simply contained an offer or allowance of $1300. However, the amount offered and its appraised value are often very different. In this case the vehicle might already have been appraised for $1700. When the customer said he would need $2000 for his vehicle, all the dealer had to do was deduct $300 from the profit of the deal. In ninety-nine out of one hundred cases, the dealer and his managers will never allow the customer to be this lucky and meet his counter-offer. You'll find the rep going back to the customer with still another offer that goes only part of the way. If I were managing this deal, I would tell the rep to offer the buyer $1800 as a trade allowance and, on the payments, increase the term to sixty months but raise the interest rate to 12 percent APR. Tell the customer that the reason for the increased rate is the fact that he needs an extended period to finance the vehicle. The new payment is now $249.88 with only $500 cash down. Be hard on the guy and if he balks this time, don't forget to offer him another vehicle with less equipment since he can't afford this one.

If this sounds cruel, it happens every day.

This time there are no smiles, no niceties, just some hard-hitting facts together with the last sentence I told the rep to repeat. The customer has gained a victory, from

his point of view, but at great cost. This kind of hard negotiating will continue because it will become a matter of
pride and principle to the buyer to be able to drive away
today and score a victory as well. But now you get to negotiate with the manager(s) because the rep has gone as
far as he can with the transaction. The counter-offers will
go back and forth for a while as the manager makes the
exhausted customer sweat just a little longer.

The situation is completely under control

Never for a moment will the manager or the salesperson
allow this sales situation to get "out of control." If the
customer ever displays any indication of walking out,
some good old-fashioned begging and pleading will take
place. Up to then the sales team will just act like astute
business people, but head for the door and you will see all
hell break loose. You'll start receiving apologies from
everyone, including the manager and even the lot attendants. Control having been lost, the sales staff will do anything to restore it. Once control is recaptured, you can
expect business as usual, and the system will once again
dictate how the players talk and act. In Chapter 5 we
discuss some foolproof methods of combating this so-called
sales system, along with any other tactic the sales team
may throw at you. This example will, I hope, serve as a
vivid warning as well as give you the motivation never to
allow yourself to be placed in a similar situation.

The appraisal

Each time the dealership appraises your trade vehicle, you
run the risk of losing hundreds of dollars. That is a harsh

statement to make, but it is true. There are so many different ways to "steal" money on your trade that no one can cover all of them. Therefore I will attempt to go over only the most common devices you will encounter.

If you have not yet completed gathering the pertinent data and prices on your trade-in, then I'm certain that when you finish reading this section you'll rush to do so. Let's assume for a moment that a 1982 Oldsmobile Cutlass Supreme Brougham is worth $3900 wholesale. In other words, this **ACV**, or Actual Cash Value, is the amount that the dealer would be willing to pay if he decided to buy the car outright. There is only one way for a manager to evaluate your vehicle: go out and look at it, take it for a test drive, figure out its worth from a used-car guide, and then deduct reconditioning costs and any other expenses that might be necessary. The market value is determined by how well your vehicle is selling and how fast it will move off the dealer's used-car lot.

There are many ways for the dealer to write down the information he collects on your vehicle. You will notice that whatever form the manager uses, it has plenty of room for such things as mechanical repairs that may be needed, body or paint finish repairs, tire conditions, windshield damage, and just about any item that will cost the dealer money in order to restore it to near-original condition. After the used-car manager or appraiser completes his evaluation and finishes filling out the form, the rep will generally stroll back to the sales manager's office and report the findings.

At this point, all is well with everyone but you, the buyer. You are anxiously awaiting the bid on your vehicle. Depending on the system they use, you may never really know the true value of your car or truck, for many dealers and their sales departments have come up with various ways of concealing your vehicle's actual worth. These mind games continue in order to keep you in the dark and off balance as much as possible regarding the car deal. For example, a common practice is this one:

Used-Car Appraisal Form

Year _____ Make _____ Model _____

Miles _____ Color _____

CONDITION AND / OR REPAIRS

XXXXXXXXXXXXXXXXXXXXXXXXXXXXXXXXXXXXXXXXXXXXXX

XXXXXXXXXXXXXXXXXXXXXXXXXXXXXXXXXXXXXXXXXXXXXX

XXXXXXXXXXXXXXXXXXXXXXXXXXXXXXXXXXXXXXXXXXXXXX

Appraised Value

X ___Joe Average_____ $3600
                              _____

Manager or Appraiser   _____

All the necessary information does appear on this form, but it looks like the dealer has made an error on the bottom of the page. We said the value of the vehicle was $3900, but as you can see, $3600 appears on this page. There is no error, however. It "really" says $3900. Each line under the price on the appraisal form represents $100; consequently, if you add to the $3600 the three lines, you get a total of $3900. It looks as if the manager merely used special emphasis when he wrote down the value of the vehicle, but it was really a code. When the rep comes back to the office and drops the form on the desk, you quickly scan it to find out the amount.

This is done for two important reasons. First, the low figure will or should get you wondering whether your car is worth less than you thought. Furthermore, if you wanted $3900, $3600 is not too far away. Second, it gives the dealer some room to move on your trade should he have to give you more money. He can go up without ever really going over the true value. You'll think he has given you more money when in fact he has given you nothing. If a good grinder talks you into believing that your vehicle is really worth only $3600 or $3700, he has just taken two or three hundred dollars out of your pocket. In view of the fact that an average commission gives the rep at least 25 percent of the profit, he would have picked up an additional $75 for only a couple of minutes' worth of grinding.

Alternatively, the value could be stated as $3500— DR. In this case, it appears as if the appraiser gave you only $3500 and that his initials follow the amount. Wrong —*D*, the fourth letter in the alphabet, represents four hundred dollars to play with, and *R* indicates that this vehicle will be a Retail unit if it is traded. In other words, the vehicle is worth going on the dealer's used-car lot as a nice piece of merchandise.

At some car stores the initials really are the manager's, so don't go nuts attempting to figure out the "system." If you have shopped around as suggested, you'll have the bank manager's opinion from the used-car guide as well as three buy bids from other used-car managers in your notes and will be able to compare the figures accordingly.

The touch method

Before your vehicle is ever evaluated or appraised, in most sales systems the rep takes you directly to your vehicle so that the information can be written down on the appraisal form. The license number, serial number, equipment, model number, and a complete description of your pride and joy are all put on the form. As the rep walks around your vehicle gathering this information, he can reach out and touch any problem areas of your car or truck. He will say nothing but will tap each area that needs attention. You realize he is picking apart your old clunker. It was a fine example of an automobile before he started, but now it is a bucket of nuts and bolts. But that is never stated. On the contrary, this entire playlet is performed entirely to give you the idea that your vehicle has problems that will cost the dealer money to repair. If the dealer is going to resell this vehicle, it is going to cost a lot of money to get it on its feet. You may find yourself trying to explain the dent or broken windshield or else apologizing for not having the time to get the problem fixed sooner. Another psychological attack on you, the buyer.

You can fool some of the people . . .

In Las Vegas or Atlantic City, the casinos go with the odds. The odds are with the house, and the house never ever loses. The same theory applies to both dealers who operate under sales systems and those who do not. The dealers with a system make it mandatory for all salespeople to follow the guidelines. The dealers without the system will use many of these same techniques but only when the situation seems to call for them. The no-system guys are looser and generally feel that their dealership has highly trained professionals who do not require the constant management supervision. Most of the time they are correct. Your "old pros" usually work at this type of establishment and are just as deadly as those who use the system. Often the larger and more sophisticated dealerships that handle more than one brand of vehicle will use a rigid system. The sales reps are almost always younger and have little or no previous automobile sales experience. This is a sure-fire method of determining whether a car store uses a system. If most of the reps appear to be under the age of thirty, you can assume that they use the TO method of sales.

Which is best for me, the buyer?

When you finish reading this book, you will not care what system the dealer employs because you will be able to use it against him with great effectiveness. So don't give it a second thought. My purpose in this chapter is to make you aware of these provocative mind games that buyers face each time they consider making a purchase. You should understand the trouble you'll be in if you're not careful, and you need to know these things if you are to use them against your opponent. What do you think about the car business now? Isn't it a bit more complex than you figured? Do you see how people like yourself wind up paying thousands more than they should?

5

Taking Control of Your Sale

What is control?

The dictionary defines *control* as "the act or power of regulating, guiding, or restraining; authority; rule or management; method of checking; regulating; to restrain or to dominate."

The major goal of a buyer is to purchase a vehicle as easily and cheaply as possible. The major goal of the dealership is to sell as many cars and trucks as possible for the largest profit. If it weren't for price, the buyer and dealer would have a marvelous relationship and live happily ever after. But since dealers must try to outsmart buyers, control is the best way to do so. If a thousand people marched on city hall and began throwing bottles and rocks, you would call them a mob; if the same people went to a ballgame but were seated while screaming and yelling, you would call them a crowd; if the same people then went to a symphony and listened attentively and then applauded with enthusiasm, you would call them an audience. It is the amount of control or social pressure that makes the difference. Therefore, when sales reps control you, they do so with the thought that the control will lead to closing the sale.

Examples of great control

The buyers who get the best deals are the most uncontroll-
able, those who do not follow reps around like puppies. I
once held an informal seminar for forty or fifty people.
During my talk, I used a couple of people in the audience
as guinea pigs. For about twenty minutes I told these two
to follow me around with signs and props that were to
assist me as I spoke. When I went to one side of the room,
they followed. I walked to the back of the room and they
followed. Not once did I refer to the charts, but the "assis-
tants" continued to follow. Everyone got the idea when I
began to jog instead of walk. Naturally, they began running to keep up. Finally, one of the subjects leaned over
and whispered to someone in the group, "This is a dumb
idea, but how are we doing so far?" They were too worried
about doing a good job for me and not making a fool of
themselves in front of forty other people to see what was
happening.

When things were slow around the dealership I would
assemble my reps on the showroom floor. For fun, I'd bet
that I could talk the next customer who walked in the door
into climbing into the trunk and shutting it for a minute,
which I proceeded to do. My presentation and control of
the customer would and could convince them to do anything. Why? To motivate my reps to sell and to show the
customer at firsthand how much room there was in the
trunk. It was a joke, but the prospect did not know and
believed that I was doing a great selling job. My reps then
told me to go back to my office while they attempted this
control trick on the next prospect.

Turn things around at the start

You've got to decide that you will do whatever it takes to get control of your sale. Don't work for the dealer. You must perform like an actor if you want to save real money. It's not hard but you must break some old habits, which may be difficult. Customers have a tendency to follow. If a rep has control, he will tell you the vehicle that interests you is over there and begin walking toward it. He will expect you to follow. Don't. Show the rep right away that you're not a follower but a leader. Never trail behind. Insist that he go to the vehicle and bring it to you while you freshen up in the rest room. Make demands! He is working for you and is in a people-pleasing business. You'll be shocked at the instant respect he'll have for you.

Be kind, be fair, but be tough! As soon as a rep approaches and greets you, tell him exactly what you want. Exactly! "I would like to see a new Chevrolet Celebrity, either white or gray with blue interior, and with factory air conditioning, automatic transmission, and a six-cylinder engine." Very direct and to the point. Then the only thing your rep can do is head in the direction of the car you requested. *Stop!* Just ask him to point out the vehicle and then be kind enough to let you look alone for a while. As soon as you finish browsing you'll come and get him. Then ask for his card, tell him your name, and stop talking. You've said enough. Go directly to the vehicle without looking back. If the rep wants to argue that he'll be glad to take you, look him in the eye and say, "Do you have a policy in this agency against permitting buyers to browse on their own for a few minutes? If so, I'd better go to (mention competitor) and see what their policy is." At this point, any rep will back up and let you have your way. Be sure to get his name and assure him that as soon as you finish browsing, you'll come and get him. Fair enough?

A small victory

You have scored a small victory and established some important ground rules. By demanding and getting your way the rep will wonder what type of person you are. This small victory should set the tone for the next skirmish. The trick here is to have some time on your own not only to look at the vehicles, but to plan your next move and survey the situation. You already know what you are shopping for, right down to the color and equipment. If you have done your homework, you already know if the vehicle you want is in stock because you've been to the agency when it was closed and you made sure. So looking now is nothing more than a period to catch your breath and plan strategy.

A picture is worth a thousand words

If you really want to shock your rep, after you get your thoughts in order, find him and ask for a "product presentation" on the car or truck you desire. He will not know how to react to that statement. You will, in fact, help him to do his job when you ask for the show. You will also skip an hour's worth of time-consuming chatter and "getting-to-know-you" conversation. As you both walk to the vehicle, ask the rep to follow you to your own vehicle because you forgot something. Then turn and head toward your vehicle. He will follow you like a puppy. When you get to your vehicle, lean in and bring out the yellowest legal pad you can find. Say nothing and start walking to the new cars. Try not to look at the rep when you make this move because you might start laughing at the expression on his face when he sees the pad.

Make sure that all your notes regarding the equipment, prices, options, colors, and any other useful information are out of sight several pages from the top. This will give you plenty of room to make new notes as well as write down questions during the rep's presentation. Have some questions ready to ask that will keep him talking and help you to listen and think about what you are doing. In addition, since a few of the answers you get are likely to be wrong or inaccurate, ask some questions to which you already know the answers to see if your rep knows what he is talking about. If he wants to be credible with you, make him earn it.

Play your own mind games

As you walk to the vehicle and prepare for the product presentation, you can turn the tide further in your favor. Tell the rep that you will not be trading your vehicle (assuming you have one to trade) but rather that you plan to sell it privately. Whether you do or not makes no difference at this point. However, the rep will begin to sell you on the basis of no trade and anything he says regarding the discount will automatically increase because he will now want to sweeten the deal by offering a higher no-trade discount. You can spring the trade on the rep later on after you get the best possible deal on the car first. During the presentation, listen, look, and observe your sales pro. Do not do a great deal of talking; do a great deal of listening. The less you say, the less likely it is that you'll give away any of your secrets. Remember, by handling the deal this way thus far, you have avoided a great deal of small talk as well as eliminated the preliminary portion of the pitch. You have moved directly to the heart of the deal, but at *your* speed and pace.

As soon as you've heard enough, stop the rep. I mean, in the middle of a sentence, just interrupt him and tell him that you would like a demonstration ride right now. (Be nice and be firm.) Because you are in control of this sale, *you* must decide when to start the next segment. This is a "controlled buying effort" on your part, so take charge and exhibit authority. Ask the rep to pull the vehicle up to the showroom while you run inside to get a drink of water. This will give you a small break in the action as well as more time to collect your thoughts. Use it and don't forget to review your notes while you have a minute or two.

Usually the rep will accompany you on the demo ride. If so, please ask the rep the following: "Sir, would you be good enough to do me a favor? Would you please drive the vehicle off the lot so I can see how it feels from a passenger's point of view?" Again, you are giving the orders and, to accommodate you, the rep should do as you ask. Simply inform the rep when you want to get behind the wheel. When you return to the dealership, make sure you park where you want to park.

These little mind games definitely have an effect on your foe. He is spending more time trying to please you than thinking of ways to get you into his back pocket. He will be off balance and in the dark as to your next move. Most customers are completely predictable. Your unprecedented behavior and strongmindedness will continue to be your best defense.

Body language

Every time you fire a command at your startled adversary, watch his movements and his expressions. For example, you may be *too* much in control. If you sense the pro becoming a bit angry or argumentative, ease off a little. If, when asking the rep a question, you find him looking down at the ground or up in the sky, he's probably lying. Most people cannot look a person in the eye and tell an untruth. When you are in the office, and the rep is restless or fidgety, this is a sign that you are putting him in a jam. Always look your opponent directly in the eye when speaking, since this will strengthen your position. Be sure you talk slowly, clearly, and calmly at all times. If you find yourself in a jam, and begin to stutter and stammer, then the rep can seize the initiative.

Ask why

Any time you develop a memory lapse and forget what to do next, simply ask "why?" While you get your detailed answer, think of the next move. In the same vein, if in the middle of negotiations things get "too hot," defuse the situation by excusing yourself and go directly to the rest room. If your spouse is with you, he or she should leave to get a drink as well. A good way to cool things off is to ask your rep to get you a soft drink or cup of coffee. While he is gone, you can review.

Share the responsibility

If you are married and the purchase is a joint effort, then both the husband and wife should share the duties of securing a great deal. Rehearse your parts and develop some private signals to use in case of problems. If one thinks all is well and the other recognizes a problem, you will want to have a silent way to communicate. Don't forget the

"Starsky and Hutch" routine. Make sure you have everything worked out before you step onto the dealer's property.

Controlled silence

If you are listening to someone speak, it is normal to make some reply once he finishes. However, if the speaker expects you to respond and you do not, then the speaker will have the overwhelming urge to continue talking in order to fill the silence. When you do not take your part in the conversation, the other person will have to carry on solo. By remaining silent, you will force the other person to continue talking. This is an excellent way to hear the rep restate his case and allows you additional time.

The more silent you are when you are being sold, the less well the rep can read you. It then goes without saying that the close will be almost impossible. Try it. The next time a friend says something that would normally bring an immediate reply from you, say nothing and see what happens.

The second baseman

The single most frustrating thing for any salesperson is to have to sell the product to two different sets of people. If a husband and wife go to an agency, the rep has a reasonable chance to talk the couple into buying. However, if a friend goes along for the ride and is present during the sale, then the rep ends up selling the vehicle twice: first to the couple, second to the friend. If you want complete control over your sale and especially want the opportunity to remove yourself from a potentially dangerous situation should one arise, then bring along a friend. If you are a single person, make certain you take a friend along.

Anyone who has ever attempted to make a purchase has made or almost made the wrong move. Telling a friend exactly what you are up to will practically guarantee that you won't get sandbagged. Give your pal some signals to use in the event you get into a jam. For example, if a rep somehow talks you into more car than you can afford, the friend could remind you of your maximum price. Or the friend could be there simply to back up anything you say or demand. Good reps will try to win a second baseman over by either complimenting or buttering him up. Make sure your friend stays loyal to you.

Don't back up

If you cannot stick to your guns, then don't walk into a dealership. There is far too much temptation and you are likely to give in to hard selling. Remember, you should know exactly what your budget is, exactly what you can afford, and exactly what vehicle with what equipment will best serve your needs. If you do your homework, you will be 100 percent better off and 80 percent through your sale before you even get there because you will walk in prepared. Then, after some old-fashioned acting and the use of a little charm and control, not to mention some shrewd maneuvering, you'll get the deal you are looking for. Above all, stay cool.

"Never ever let them see you sweat" is a line on a TV commercial advertising an antiperspirant. It also embodies the code you live and die by in a dealership. If you get mad, it generally means that someone pushed a button you didn't like. Cool the situation off by walking away for a moment. If the going gets too tough, recognize it and defuse the tension. If the price is too high, or the trade allowance is ridiculous, defuse. You can always say, "Wait a second!" You can always say, "No, I'm sorry, but I can't do that today." Never let anyone get the best of you. And if someone does, never let him know it.

Say exactly what you mean

If you want to stay in control, then do not pull any punches. When something strikes you wrong, it probably is. Therefore speak up and stop the proceedings and don't allow them to move ahead until you are satisfied all is well. Do it even if you have to get a bit rude because if you wait, later might be too late. I'm not suggesting that you start calling names, but I do suggest that no matter how it comes out of your mouth, do not allow things to go further. If your rep is trying to make you believe that a four-cylinder engine will pull your houseboat over the Rockies, demand proof. That is all you need to do.

Which type are you?

In my opinion, there are only three types of people in this world. Those who make things happen, those who wait for things to happen, and those who wonder what happened. Why wonder or wait for something to happen when it's easy to make it happen? If you do not do your homework, if you do not take the time to get some buy bids on your trade, if you don't take time to call your banker, and if you don't do some comparison phone shopping, then you'll end up at the dealership with the gun in your hand loaded with blanks. It will make a noise but that's all, only noise. In

the next chapter, we get down and dirty. It's time to separate the makers from the waiters, to put our money where
our mouth is. In other words, are we going to buy or not?
I believe that when we finish the negotiations for your
vehicle the price will be so cheap, some might say we
stole it.

6

The Art of Negotiating
Your Purchase

In negotiating the purchase of a new or used motor vehicle, it's every man for himself. The dealer wants to sell another unit and make money, the manager wants to win a contest and make money, the service manager wants the agency to sell more units so his mechanics can service more which will make money, the salesperson wants to sell another unit so that he can keep his job, win the volume award, win the sales award, and make money. In fact, everyone at the dealership is totally dependent on selling as many cars and trucks as possible. The buyer simply wants to buy a vehicle and save some money while doing so. Each side has opposite goals.

I'm tough, I'm hard

It is fair to say that if you know where you want to go, then it is reasonable to plan the route that will take you there. If you lived in New York City and wanted to drive to Los Angeles, you would have to plan many things: which road gets you there quickest, how many miles you can travel in one day, and where you would sleep each evening, not to mention how much money it will cost.

Why can't you do the same when it comes to your transportation purchases? You know what you want and if you use the work sheets in the glossary, you can figure your monthly payments to the penny. If you plan to pay cash for the entire sale, you know better than anybody else what you can afford. So what's the problem? Did I hear you say that when you've bought in the past the prices were always too high? Guess what? The rep, and the managers, are trained to start at the highest possible price. After all, if I was a rep and started at the actual invoice price, you wouldn't believe me anyway. You would expect and demand that the price be reduced because I must have a little more room to maneuver.

It never fails—customers get themselves into a closing office and try to outfox the fox. The rep says, "Well, Mr. Smith, I'll bet this vehicle is exactly what you're looking for. Now comes the tough part, sir. All we have to do is figure out how much you'll pay today. Mr. Smith, what can I sell you this car for today?" Most reps will say something like this. And the reply is invariable. If I had a dollar for every time a consumer answered, "I want to pay as little as possible, so sharpen your pencil and give me your rock-bottom deal," I'd be a rich man today.

Let's do this right. We will use the following figures:

Factory (MSRP) Sticker Retail Price	$11,478.80

The following list is from a supplementary window sticker:
Dealer-added equipment

Paint protection treatment __	$ 399.00
Undercoating _____	169.95
Interior care treatment _____	89.95
Body side molding _____	79.95
Accent pinstripes _____	82.50
Vinyl roof (padded) _____	225.00
Remove AM radio for credit _	− (90.00)
Install AM/FM stereo and cassette _____	495.00
Dealer preparation fee _____	75.00
Total of dealer adds _____	$ 1,526.35
Total retail selling price _____	$13,005.15

While we're here, let's figure cost. I mean real cost! In Chapter 7 you'll find the real cost of many items, including a formula to use for calculating what the dealer pays for his vehicles. Using those numbers, here we go.

RETAIL STICKER	$11,478.80
LESS APPROXIMATE INVOICE (*see pages 100–102*)	−$10,157.52
POTENTIAL PROFIT OR MARKUP FROM THE FACTORY	$ 1,321.28

APPROXIMATE REAL COST OF DEALER-ADDED OPTIONS

Option	Retail	Real Cost
Paint protection	$ 399.00	$ 50.00
Undercoating	169.95	25.00
Interior care	89.95	25.00
Body molding	79.95	25.00
Accent stripes	82.50	35.00
Vinyl roof	225.00	140.00
AM/FM cassette	495.00	395.00
AM radio credit	(−90.00)	(−90.00)
Dealer prep	75.00	0
	$1,526.35	$ 605.00

$ 1,526.35
$ −605.00

921.35 Potential profit in adds
+1,321.28 = Potential profit from car
$ 2,242.28 = Total markup or potential profit on this vehicle

Never ever think of purchasing a vehicle with more than $200 worth of dealer-added options. The only dealer-added items you should ever consider are body side moldings and possibly accent stripes. That's it. The others will simply run up the price, as in the example above. By doing a bit of comparison shopping you'll get the same product for less money elsewhere without any hassle. The mere thought of spending $399 for paint sealant, which costs the dealer only $70 to install, should send you running to the auto specialty shops in your area. In the example, I gave the radio the benefit of the doubt. The stereo cassette might have cost only $150, depending on the quality of the set. Shop around, save some money.

Well, you've just made that brilliant statement: I want to pay as little as possible, so sharpen your pencil and give me your rock-bottom deal." What do you think the rep will do next? The rep will always make the first move by popping the question of price. Although you anticipate it, each time it comes, you fall into the same trap. As soon as you tell him to give you his best price, he will. My next response to you, the buyer, would be something like this, "OK, Mr. Smith, the owner of the dealership allows me to discount this vehicle $250, and since you seem to be a nice man, I'll go ahead and give you the whole $250 right now. It is all yours, sir. Fair enough, Mr. Smith?" Poor Mr. Smith, who was expecting to hear at least $1000 to start with, is stunned.

You've got to be smarter than Mr. Smith. You recall that the trip from New York to Los Angeles would go much better with a well-thought-out plan and budget as a first step. Do the same thing here—plan. Don't attempt to purchase without a knowledge of price and price structure. Do your homework and come up with cost figures, as I did. Now, since you know the approximate cost (it could be off by $100 either way), decide what you are willing to pay the dealer in dollars including a profit. Be fair. Is one, two, three, or maybe five hundred dollars a fair profit? You must decide *before* you get to the agency. If you wait until you're there, the rep might influence your final decision. Let's give the dealership $200 profit on this deal. Thus:

$10,157.52	approx. dealer cost on vehicle
605.00	approx. dealer cost on adds
$10,762.52	approx. dealer cost
200.00	dealer profit
$10,962.52	price we are willing to pay

If you suppose that having arrived at this wonderful figure you are now able to start negotiating, you are dead wrong. If your plan is to be effective, you'll have to leave room to "give in" a few times; if you start there, you'll start too high. I would offer the rep . . . Wait! Let's return to the examples. You've already made the dumb request that he give you his rock-bottom price. You are, therefore, still in space and by now are somewhere near Jupiter.

As soon as you are seated in a comfortable closing office, the rep will pop the question. When he does, you must really go into your act. Like this: "Well, Mr. Smith, what can I sell you this car for today?" *You* say, "That is a good question, and I want you to know that I haven't taken it lightly. I believe you are a fine representative and a credit to this organization. I plan to tell your boss about the good job you've done here today as well. Indeed, it is because of you and your help that I will offer exactly $9638.57 . . . plus tax and license fee, of course." Then total silence on your part.

No, I haven't lost my mind. You've offered them a deal which is more than one thousand dollars under cost. You have answered the question and made a legitimate offer. The rep will be speechless. Instead of waiting and allowing him to make you a ridiculous offer, you have made something happen by beating him to the punch. Earlier, when the rep offered a $250 discount, you would have responded hotly as you told him no. Then he would have given you the other barrel of the shotgun: "Well, Mr. Smith, if you won't accept my offer of a $250 discount, then how much more will you have to get?" He would have forced you to come up with a figure. The fact he has offered you so little will intimidate you and cause you to come up in price.

Here you have turned the tables; you are now in the driver's seat. What can he do? He may hem and haw, but he will write it up because his training dictates it. Making

an offer that is $1000 under cost will afford us the oppor-
tunity to let them **"bump"** us several times. Once we approach the price we are willing to pay, as we go through
their gang of expert closers, a simple strong statement will
complete our work. "Sir, I appreciate your position, but
you will have to appreciate mine even more. As you can
see, I have increased my offer several times, by your own
request for me to do so, and gentlemen, let me make this
perfectly clear. I want to buy a car here, and I think you'll
agree with the fact I am trying. I've come up about one
thousand dollars, and I would call that trying. I guess I
could be at the wrong car agency. My final offer is
$10,962.52, or I'll just have to drive over to (name compet-
itor) and make them the same offer." (Shut up and do not
say another word.)

To review: First, by starting low and allowing them to
raise your bid, you've let them "earn" several small victo-
ries. The manager will think to himself that you are "reasonable" in that you did end up giving $1000 more. He will
think he's done a good job in trying to close the sale and
might be embarrassed to pursue additional bumps. (After
all, you can only go so far.) Second, using the threat of
going to a competitor will make him want the deal even
more because he certainly does not want to have gone
through this ordeal only to have you buy elsewhere. This
time it will be the manager and rep who will be faced with
making the decision instead of you. You will be doing the
grinding, you will have them backed up against the wall.
Either the boss says yes, or you make the same offer to
their competition: these are the alternatives. Believe me,
under these circumstances you'll have it your way and pay
the price you want to pay every time.

Negotiating with odd numbers

Did you notice the odd figure we used when making our first offer? $9638.57 is certainly not a round number. If we had offered $9600 or $9700, it might imply that we would be willing to go higher. However, $9638.57 specifies the amount you are willing to pay down to the exact penny. It sounds final as well as firm. If the rep asks you how you arrived at this particular figure, reply that is both what you can afford and what your research leads you to believe is fair. This answer is not merely simple and clear, it has further implications. Each time you allow yourself to be bumped in the ensuing negotiations, you can use the budgeted amount as your emergency escape route. "Well, sir, I don't know, I'll have to give this some thought because I'm already nearly a thousand dollars higher than my budget will allow." Making this statement will reinforce your position. Moreover, the use of such odd figures will really make them believe you've done your homework. In addition, each time you increase the bid, go up by another odd amount; it will keep them off balance.

Traditional sentences

Many people in the car business use language forcefully —phrases such as "Is our price a fair one?" "Would you buy today if I could . . . ," "Tell me what I have to do to earn your business," "What will it take . . . ," and the list goes on. Almost every sentence will end with the word *today!* The entire sales procedure is to get you to take action now—not tomorrow or next week, but today. I suggest that it would be wise to use this word, *today,* in your pitch too. For example, "I'll buy right now, today, if your boss will approve my offer." Or, "Mr. Manager, I see you're not interested in selling a vehicle today, and I must purchase now, so I'll have to withdraw my offer and submit it to (name competition) and see if they will sell me something today." The use of the odd numbers, the low beginning bid, and statements like these are designed to make your point effectively. Since the dealers and managers resort to many of these same mind games, it is only right to give them a dose of their own medicine.

The final option

When everything is finally agreed to and you know exactly what the price will be, then as innocently as you can, look the rep in the eye and tell him you've just decided to trade in your vehicle. You simply don't want to bother with selling it privately. However, what you end up getting in trade might affect your ability to buy today. The astonished salesperson will ask how much you had in mind. Tell him a figure that is $500 more than your best buy bid. Let him have it appraised, and then do some old-fashioned horse trading, or else sell it to the dealer who has given you the best bid. That way you will know beyond any doubt you got the best price on your trade. Remember, you can always sell it privately if you have the time and patience. Make sure, when you have it appraised, that it is spotless both inside and out.

A word on foreign vehicles

I don't know who started the rumor that when you buy a foreign vehicle, you get no discount off sticker price. This is pure bull. People who purchase foreign cars are supposed to be more educated, more intelligent, more astute, more everything; in my opinion, any buyer of a foreign vehicle who accepts this no-discount myth is one of the biggest fools walking on the planet. The mistaken impression that you are buying a better car or truck because it is foreign and the stupidity of believing what you are being told add up to the most amazing con job ever attempted. I'm sorry to be so brutally frank, but I've seen many people pay thousands more than they should have just because it's a foreign product. We can discuss the pros and cons of the way Americans manufacture vehicles far into the night, but the facts are clear. In recent years GM, Ford, Chrysler, and AMC have pulled out all of the stops and are building much better cars. In my opinion, the follow-up programs used by the U.S. manufacturers to insure that your car is operating properly and that you are satisfied with its performance, style, and engineering are second to none. Sure, years ago the factories were lax and produced inferior products, but today, American-made vehicles are more than equal to the competition. The German Mercedes-Benz and perhaps the English Jaguar and BMW autos are the only foreign products (and Jaguar only in the last few years) that consistently outperform everyone. The fact that you must spend $35,000 to $60,000 for some of these vehicles may have a bearing on how they are built. (I sure hope so for that kind of money.) So unless you have fifty big ones burning a hole in your pocket, consider buying an American car or truck. But if you still insist on buying a foreign car, follow the same steps: do your homework, do your research, and go in and make something happen. Incidentally, on foreign cars and especially trucks, watch that supplementary sticker. You'll find that it is marked up considerably. You might get a discount and still pay more than window sticker. Don't do it. You'll be sorry. Paying over window sticker doesn't make sense at all. And I repeat, compare what you get in a foreign job to an American beauty. You may be surprised.

You can always let them cook a bit longer

Consider this analogy: in preparing a Thanksgiving turkey, the great chefs look for a young tender tom turkey that will taste great and will be done when everyone is ready to eat. However, occasionally the cook will come upon an old tough bird that will simply have to remain in the oven a little longer before it is done. No matter how long the bird cooks, however, the results are the same, and the chef ends up with a feast fit for a king. The point is that sometimes one must be patient in order to get the best results. If you as a car buyer do run into a situation that is not going as planned, *stop*. As soon as you sense that negotiations are beginning to falter, and you've run into a tough old bird, reconsider making a new offer only at home. I will bet that as soon as you head for your car, things will change. And if they don't right then and there, be prepared to get a lot of phone calls from that dealership.

Once you make an offer, stick to it. Don't let them continue bumping you over your actual buying price. You can always accept the offer the next day. These managers are highly trained and will let you stew and simmer for a while too. If you plan to play this game, then be a player and stand pat. The rep has your telephone number; once everyone at the dealership believes that you've really reached your limit, you'll receive a call. Patience!

7

Tactical
Maneuvering

Preparation and timing

The best athletes in the world prepare before any contest.
They will do whatever it takes, mentally and physically,
to insure they are ready to meet the challenge. Then there
are the losers, the second-place finishers, the fourth place,
the tenth place, and so on. To be second means that you
still lose. In the game of cars, unless you come in first, the
dealer and his staff win. This is the only way to look at it.
If he wins, you pay too much. If you win, you pay your
price, not his.

To prepare you further, the next few pages will serve
as reminder, as guideline, as checklist, and as motivator.
Not only do I want you to make a great deal, but I want
you to have confidence in your ability to make that deal.
If you are going to proceed flawlessly through the sale, you
must know that your information is accurate. If your figures are on the money, then your words will be more force-
ful.

[96

What I Must Accomplish Before I Make My Deal

Review the following checklist to make certain you haven't forgotten anything. Answer all questions honestly.

	YES	NO
1. Do I really need a new(er) vehicle?	____	____
2. Do I know what my driving needs are?	____	____
3. Do I have a specific vehicle in mind?	____	____
4. Will this vehicle serve my needs?	____	____
5. Will it meet the needs of my family?	____	____
6. Will the gas mileage be adequate?	____	____
7. Will my current vehicle be traded?	____	____
8. Will I sell it privately for more?	____	____
9. Have I completed the form in Chapter 2 regarding improvements to my present vehicle?	____	____
10. Would making the repairs accomplish my goal, thus extinguishing my need for new transport?	____	____
11. Did I complete the building-my-car form in Chapter 2?	____	____
12. Do I know which options I want and whether I can afford them?	____	____
13. Did I do my telephone shopping to learn prices on dealer-installed items?	____	____
14. Have I called my banker for the "book value" of my trade vehicle?	____	____
15. Did I obtain from the banker the following information: current interest rates at bank and approximate payments on $_____ and on $_____, if I decide to let the bank handle my loan?	____	____

What I Must Accomplish Before I Make My Deal
(continued)

	YES	NO
16. Have I stopped at the car agency to pick up product brochures?	_____	_____
17. Have I obtained three buy bids for my trade vehicle?	_____	_____
18. Do I know if the car store where I want to buy has a sales "system"?	_____	_____
19. Do I know why I am choosing this dealer first?	_____	_____
20. Have I checked the paper and media ads to see who is advertising the most?	_____	_____
21. Do I know which factory incentives are currently being offered on the car I intend to purchase?	_____	_____
22. Do I realize I can get a better deal by waiting until the end of the month?	_____	_____
23. Have I contacted my insurance agent to see how much my rates may increase?	_____	_____
24. Have I completed the personal financial statement in Chapter 2 to insure that I can afford this purchase?	_____	_____
25. Have I arrived at the tentative price of my vehicle and have I double-checked my calculations?	_____	_____
26. Have I figured my monthly payments by using the chart in the glossary?	_____	_____
27. Do I understand all the terms in the glossary?	_____	_____
28. Has my spouse (or second baseman) reviewed all this material and have we practiced exactly what we're going to do and say?	_____	_____

What I Must Accomplish Before I Make My Deal
(continued)

	YES	NO

29. Have we worked out an emergency escape plan?

30. Have we worked out a few silent signals for passing information?

31. Have I purchased the yellowest legal pad I can find?

32. Do I have my notes, prices, questions, and other data *neatly* written on my pad?

33. If I still owe on my trade vehicle, do I have an accurate payoff balance and did I use this in figuring my purchase?

34. Do I know what the rep's first sentence will be when I go to the car store?

35. Have I reread this book to insure my victory at the dealership?

36. On the day that I visit the agency, will my trade vehicle be spotless?

37. Do I remember that if I get into a jam, I should *stop* the proceedings, get some refreshments, and think about what is happening?

38. Do I have my first offer firmly in my mind; is it about $1000 under the approximate dealer cost?

39. Do I remember that I should assume nothing and get everything promised in writing?

40. Will I exercise patience and be ready to walk out and let them cook a bit longer if necessary?

$$. Am I ready to meet the enemy head on, and am I mentally prepared to make my deal happen, today?

A formula for calculating the dealer's factory invoice

One of the biggest problems customers face is not knowing what the car or truck actually costs the dealer. Buyers don't even have a clue as to approximate markups on these expensive products. A customer once told me that on a $15,000 vehicle the dealer made $5000, the factory made $5000, and the mechanics and yours truly cut up the remaining $5000. Other customers believe the markup on a new unit was 25 to 35 percent; they, too, are wrong. A Rolls-Royce may have a $15,000 or $20,000 markup, and a $50,000 Mercedes might have $10,000 profit built into the sticker price, but the American cars and trucks most people buy will average between 10 and 20 percent. For example, a new Chevy Camaro may have a recommended selling price (MSRP) of $13,560 with no dealer adds. This represents about a 13 percent markup from the $12,000 invoice. Here's how it's calculated: $12,000 (the invoice price) multiplied by 113 percent (13 percent above and beyond the $12,000) gives you $13,560. That's a profit of $1,560 if the dealer sold you the car at full window sticker and installed no options.

This figure may not seem large, but when you consider where else profit can be made, you'll see the full picture. The example in Chapter 6 showed the dealer installing over $1500 worth of extras that actually cost him slightly over $600. By doing so, the dealer increased the profit from $1560 to over $2100. If the dealer makes another $300 on your trade, you're up over $2400. Then he sells you a warranty and makes another couple of hundred, and you buy some life and disability insurance on the contract, which produces at least $200 more. Now you are at a potential profit of over $2800 and you're still not done. He makes money on the financing—most do—

and then turns around and sells your used car to someone for another $1500, and you have not yet visited the service department.

Once you grasp the fact the dealer has the opportunity to make this kind of profit a couple of hundred times each and every month, then you will understand why he is in the car business. If the price you pay includes more than a $3000 markup and the rep convinced you he could give you only a $1400 discount, ask yourself this question again: how long will it take you to earn the other $1600?

Study the figures on the next page, and remember that the dealer does need to make a profit. But let him make what *you* determine is fair, not what he asks you for. The percentages are accurate to about 1 percent either way, depending on the car or truck.

Frankly speaking

Before you picked up this book, you were a novice when it came to car buying. I don't care how many cars you purchased before, but from now on things are going to be different. Never again will you fear getting ripped off by a slick dealer and his staff. Now that you have all this material at your disposal and know exactly what to do, it will be almost impossible for you to make a "bad " car deal in the future. Right? Wrong! It's not that easy.

Just like anything else, to be good at something requires a little dedication, a little thought, and some good old-fashioned grit. To read this book and then fall back into the same poor buying habits will accomplish absolutely nothing. You have to have the guts to go after what you want. If your investment in this book pays off, it could

The Formula for Calculating Dealer Invoice
(± 1%)

RETAIL PRICE (MSRP)	APPROXIMATE PERCENTAGE MARKUP
$ 4,000–10,000	10
$10,000–12,000	11
$12,000–19,999	13
$20,000–26,000	16
$26,000–35,000	18
$35,000–50,000	20
over $50,000	20 +

NOTE: Do not add the dealer-installed options to the Msrp. To figure invoice amount, use only the total Msrp.

The Cost of Various Dealer-Installed Options

NOTE: This is a guide, based on fifteen years in the car business; the actual cost will vary from dealer to dealer and city to city. Remember, this is the "cost" of the option installed without markup.

OPTION	COST INSTALLED	RETAIL VALUE
1. Paint sealant treatment	$ 50	$ 300–1000
2. Interior fabric care	25	100–195
3. Undercoating	25	59–199
4. Rustproofing	75	89–599
5. Mirror glaze wax	35	99–159
6. Body side molding	25	79–139
7. Accent stripe (car)	30	79–159
8. Accent stripe (truck)	30	89–159
9. Accent stripe fancy (truck)	50	199–399
10. Accent stripe painted (car)	40	139–199
11. Door-edge guard molding	5	29–99
12. Full vinyl roof (padded)	140	225–299
13. Half-vinyl landau roof (padded)	130	199–299
14. Electric sun/moon glass roof	950	1300–1595
15. Electric sun roof (no glass)	700	999–1199
16. Pop-up or flip-up roof	150	499–799
17. T-top or glass panels	775	995–1295
18. Extra window tinting (2 dr.)	65	99–199
19. Extra window tinting (4 dr.)	75	129–199
20. Extra window tinting (wagon)	95	299–399
21. Change vinyl seats to cloth	125	399–499
22. Floor mats FR & RR (carpeted)	35	50–99
23. Floor mats FR & RR (rubber)	20	39–59
24. Interior carpeting (truck)	59	99–199
25. Air conditioning (cars and trucks)	550	650–799
26. Real spare tire (depends on brand)	75	139–199
Wheel for real spare	40	79–99
27. Extra fuel tank	140	199–299
28. Simulated wire wheel covers (set of 4)	150	199–299

The Cost of Various Dealer-Installed Options (continued)

OPTION	COST INSTALLED	RETAIL VALUE
29. Cruise control with resume	135	199–299
30. Power trunk release	25	99–199
31. Rear window louvers	75	199–299
32. Custom mag wheels (set of 4)	200	399–599
33. Mud and snow tires (set of 4)	200	399–499
34. Electronic burglar alarm (depending on quality)	95	299–499
35. AM/FM stereo w/cassette player/radio equipment	150 (low) **to** 500 (high)	299–599 **to** 600–999

NOTE: Depends on quality and brand. An average AM/FM stereo cassette player may vary $500. Check local shops and compare.

36. Power antenna	125	199–299

NOTE: The cost of some of these extras will depend on size, brand, and labor. The figures here represent approximate cost for items installed in the Southwestern United States. Prices may vary in your part of the country. Before you make your purchase, shop and compare.

reward you with a multi-thousand-dollar dividend in savings on your next purchase.

Knowing what the car salesman knows will certainly give you an edge; however, he gets to practice his craft every day of the year. Thus, if you are going to be a great car buyer, you must be fully prepared, which means knowing the prices, knowing the games reps play, knowing where to start and stop, knowing your budget, knowing how much your trade is worth, knowing how to "take charge," and knowing how to say "no" but leave the door open.

Effective negotiation is an art—the art of knowing

how to sell your idea, the art of moving gracefully in and out of troubled areas, the art of knowing when to be silent and when to be audacious, the art of being shameless as well as fearless. Just having the facts and figures before you isn't enough. To guarantee success you must appreciate the ability of the people that you are going up against. If you underestimate them or the situation, you are dead.

Selling the sizzle

What do you sell first, the sizzle or the steak? If you ask that question to a hundred car reps, they will unanimously say, "You sell the sizzle first." Why? Did you ever drive past one of those steak houses and get a whiff of the juicy cut of beef cooking over the charcoal? Although the grill in fact requires the ventilation, isn't it convenient that the fans are blowing the great aroma right to our car as we pass by? I get hungry just thinking about food. This is called selling the sizzle. It smells so good that we've got to pull over and have one.

Professional car salespeople will often sell the car so subtly that you'll end up driving home before you know what hit you. They are pros and know how to do tactical maneuvering themselves. The best way to counter a tactical move is to anticipate it. If you can "control" the sale, all the while allowing your counterpart to believe that he has complete dominance over you, then you will definitely have your opponent in checkmate.

. . . .

8

Don't Let This Happen to You!

I heard the other day

"Did you hear about; isn't it a shame about what happened to poor old. . . ?" It seems as if we constantly hear of people getting swindled out of their life savings. I have heard there is even a school somewhere that will teach you the art of ripping someone off. When someone starts a sentence with, "Say, did you hear about," I always wonder whether the story will be about me someday. I hope not. Unfortunately, I am in the position to tell you a few stories about people who played the game and lost. The sad thing, though, is they may not even know they lost. For a salesman the highest achievement is to tear off someone's head and not have him realize it. If the victim ever finds out, you may have to endure a lot of yelling and screaming as well as the threat of lawsuits, so the professional will sell with such overwhelming enthusiasm that the victim will never doubt his word or check his integrity.

You are now saying to yourself that this guy's gone overboard on this subject. Maybe, but maybe not. Perhaps a swindle to you is when someone pays a few thousand for some good bottom land only to find out it's at the bottom of a lake. This is not an indictment of the car business, for there are many fine and reputable dealers who are in business to make money, just like everyone else, but who are not insanely greedy and amoral. There are, however, a few crooks in the car business, as in every other business. Remember that the people in the sales departments of car agencies across the United States have a duty to their employer, the dealer, to make as many sales for as much profit as possible. Therefore, these horror stories you are about to hear come from people like me, who did a job and did it well. The reason I'm elaborating on the subject is to prepare some of you for a little shock. Some of these stories may hit home because you may have been the victim yourself and never knew, until now. If so, accept it and resolve never to let it happen again.

The case of the finance office bump

I wish I had a dime for each time I heard a finance manager proclaim victory. Customers will drop their guard when it's time to sign the mountain of paperwork. After the buyer goes through the anguish and has finally made the correct decision, he sits back, relaxes, and thinks about driving this shiny new vehicle home. As the rep congratulates him on making a splendid move, the manager approves the deal by placing his name next to the customer's signature and the happy buyer is whisked away to meet the person who will conclude the transaction—the finance manager.

Their defenses down, and in the presence of the new manager, the buyers, who just spent hours of torture to get the best possible deal, will throw it away in about fifteen minutes. They do not realize that they present another selling opportunity for the dealership by a well-trained professional. This time the finance person, who is likely to be a woman, has had formal training as well as on-the-job experience. Often finance managers will be college grads and may never have sold cars, but will have gone through a few weeks of training at a finance school. Dealers spend thousands to make sure their finance people have the latest training and sales techniques at their disposal, and for good reason. Depending on the size of the store, some of these departments can make as much as $100,000 each month. A dealer with monthly sales of 150 units will generally average $50,000 in finance income profit.

In a manner often smoother than the sales rep who has just sold the vehicle, the finance manager will systematically work his or her way through the following: securing the highest possible interest rate (except when factory rates are available and the buyer qualifies) because every point the finance manager gets you to pay means more profit; getting you to buy the credit life insurance and disability insurance, again making extra money; getting you to buy an extended warranty; and, depending on the dealer, some finance managers may even try to sell you additional equipment. All in all, a very profitable department.

I have handled many deals where the buyers were so happy to make a purchase that they would have agreed to anything. I wish I could tell you these were isolated incidents, but in fifteen years in the business, the story I'm about to tell you probably happened two or three hundred times. Young buyers anxious to get the deal over with will almost always pay too much for the vehicle. Then they enter the finance office not knowing what is about to take place. The expert finance manager, usually with a computer, will punch in some numbers and naturally will offer a first payment loaded with everything including the kitchen sink. The payment will incorporate the highest possible rate of interest, joint life and disability insurance, the longest available warranty, and it will all be figured at the maximum number of days before the first payment is due. (You probably don't know that if you go beyond a thirty-day first payment, it will cost a few dollars more each month to extend to forty-five days before the first payment.) If the buyers accept the payment, the manager will push a button on the computer, and the machine will produce a contract in 15 or 20 seconds. Then a couple of signatures and you're off in your new car. Easy as pie.

I've seen payments vary by as much as $100 per month. Just imagine what you could do with another $100 a month, or $6000 over a sixty-month contract. People end up creating a hardship for themselves by taking on payments that are $30, $50, or even $75 or $100 more than they can afford, all because a finance manager didn't fully disclose the terms and conditions of the contract and the customer just "stared" at the contract and did not read it. If you can't keep up and the bank is forced to repossess your vehicle, it goes on your credit report and you don't get to buy on credit again for a long time. The consequences of the bank "popping your ride" sometimes lead to financial disaster.

The case of the upside-down buyer

When a buyer is upside-down in his deal, there is an outstanding amount still owed on the current vehicle that will be carried over to the balance of the new unit; both amounts are then combined to form a new loan that will be greater than the value of the new vehicle being purchased. To put it in simple words, you've just paid the dealer for the car, the tax, the license, the documents, the dealer's profit on the new vehicle, and then you've allowed them to add the balance on your old car on top of the new one. You will always owe more than the car is worth anyway, but when you add the tax, profit, and your old balance, you'll never get out from under.

Most of the time banks will not permit you to get upside-down because, if they did, it would be impossible for them to own sufficient equity if forced to "pop" your vehicle. If the balance owed is greater than the car's real value, should the bank decide to repossess, it can only run up unnecessary legal expenses, which are simply added to the balance. The bank cannot win, and banks want to have at least a chance to break even.

This brings us to credit unions. Many of the credit unions in the United States lend their members money that represents deposits made by many of the same members. Often, the credit union will accept a greater risk or liability than a bank because the borrower is a member of the credit union. Too often the credit union will carry balances of old vehicles over to new loans just because the borrower is a member. It's great for the customer, and the credit union could not care less because the employee isn't likely to default. The buyer can continue to make mistakes, and the credit union will keep burying him deeper and deeper into debt.

I knew many customers who were way upside-down and buried in their vehicles, yet their credit union continued to finance new purchases. Some buyers would buy a new car each year or whenever the feeling moved them. But one day it all catches up. Whenever the credit union manager leaves or gets replaced, or when the credit union's loans are audited by someone with bank experience, all hell breaks loose and the credit union adopts more reasonable lending practices. The credit union tries to be good to its borrowers, who are its members, but this kind of loan is no favor. The crime here is simple. The borrower ends up with his entire paycheck going toward paying off the new purchase as well as one or more old ones that were never paid off and were carried over. When most of your check is consumed by credit-union deductions, and the mortgage and utilities, not to mention food, are still due, what happens then? I knew a man who was in this situation. He lost his house and car, and then his wife left him, all because the jerk was upside-down in his purchases and people continued to finance new automobile purchases for him. He learned his lesson in the hardest possible way.

The case of the overloaded truck

Federal law (which can be changed if enough people complain) requires monroney labels to be affixed to the windows of cars; there is no such requirement for trucks. All trucks come with the labels, but most dealers remove them so the MSRP cannot be determined. Some of the more respectable and reputable agencies elect to leave them on, but most do not.

This practice is general because on many occasions a buyer wants to trade a vehicle, usually a truck, and expects much more for the trade than it is really worth. Since the sales reps are there to accommodate and assist buyers in consummating a purchase, reps will create whatever selling price is needed to get the job done.

For example, a buyer stops in to look at a new truck and happens to have his trade with him. The rep takes one look at this relic and jacks up the price of the new truck. Let's say the truck was priced at $9600 on the missing label, but anticipating that his customer will want at least $2000 in trade and expect another grand in discount, the rep makes sure to leave a bit more room and tells his customer proudly that he can pick up this new pickup for only $13,200 if he acts quickly. The buyer, who figured his old unit was worth around $1000 (he figured less than the rep thought he would), now raises his sights another $500 and hopes he can talk the guy into allowing a big discount. After some conversation, the pro pops the question: what will it take to do a deal? The buyer instructs the rep to make him the best deal possible, so the rep takes his best shot. "Mr. Prospect, I may be able to allow you around $2500, but you will have to buy now." The buyer thinks his salesman is nuts but quickly says put it in writing. The sales pro has definitely hit the hot button because the customer has jumped at the offer. A little more game playing, and this will end up being a terrific deal—for the house and rep.

It's not easy to review what happened. How can we determine the factory invoice, lacking a window sticker to work from? A good rule of thumb is take whatever price you're quoted and deduct a full 20 percent. Banks or lease companies will allow the dealer to mark up any truck up to 20 percent from invoice. You can rest assured that if you don't see a factory label, they have marked it up the full 20 percent. But wait! Some quick math reveals that this vehicle is marked up even more than 20 percent. It happens every day. Let's go on and I'll tell you what happens.

This buyer only wants $2500, and a good pro can work the guy down a few hundred more if he tries. Assuming, however, that our truck rep is not a good grinder, he ends up allowing the customer the full $2500. The man's trade-in was appraised for only $800 by the used-car manager. The buyer agrees and makes the purchase. Question: how much profit did the dealer make on the sale? Remember, this unit was marked up well over the usual 20 percent.

Did the buyer really get what he wanted? If you recall, he only wanted $1500 in trade and hoped for a good discount. The buyer was trying to be fair and reasonable. The rep guessed the buyer would want a bundle and marked everything up enough so that he could agree to that request. However, the request for a huge trade-in never came. The buyer still got more than he wanted to begin with, and the buyer is happy and the rep is ecstatic.

The $13,200 selling price is marked up 37.5 percent over the actual MSRP of $9,600. And from the table on page 102, we know this $9,600 represents a ten percent markup from the real invoice of about $8,727.

Selling Price	$13,200
Less Trade Allowance	− 2,500
Difference	$10,700
Plus ACV of Trade	+ 800
Total Money Taken In	$11,500
Less Dealer Invoice	− 8,727
Net Dealer Profit	$ 2,773

In this example, the buyer got what he wanted, and the dealer still made $2,773 in profit!

If the buyer had known what he was doing, he might have made a deal where the agency made only $860 in profit—which is still too high in my opinion. That is, the buyer could have saved a whopping $2,000. Assuming he financed the entire amount, let's figure how much more that $2000 actually cost the buyer each month. In this case we will give the buyer a 10 percent APR for forty-eight months. From the charts in the glossary our conversion money factor is .2547, so the equation is:

$$\$2000 \times .2547 = \$50.94$$

Therefore, by not shopping around, the buyer will pay $50.94 more each month for the next forty-eight months, or $50.94 × 48 = $2445.12 in total payments. So it costs the buyer $445.12 to finance the $2000 for forty-eight months. How long will it take the guy to earn $2445.12? This can happen when purchasing a car as well. You could get what you want and get laid away too. The choice is yours.

A buyer who thought he could outfox the fox

This is a cute little true story of a buyer who decided to play both ends against the middle. A customer came into the dealership to look at a fairly expensive American sedan. As luck would have it, we had exactly what he was looking for, right down to the color. My sharp rep told me that he had a buyer and that as soon as he let the fish play himself out, he'd reel him in. Needless to say, we had a pretty sweet deal. After a little wheeling and dealing, our buyer drove away in his new car. When a manager gets a healthy (that is, very profitable) deal he always checks to make sure all the t's are crossed and the i's are dotted. In case the customer goes home and develops a case of buyer's remorse, it's nice to know that every bit of paperwork is in order. Sometimes we would go so far as to get the customer's credit approved on a "rush" basis and then send a runner down to cash the contract and collect our money.

As luck would have it, on the way home from buying our car, the customer passed another competitor that handled the same line of cars as we did. Again the customer saw the same car with almost the identical equipment. The sales rep at the other store, thinking this guy may not have finalized the deal at our agency, stepped up and took his best shot. By the time he finished his pitch, the buyer felt like a sap. The other rep had convinced him that we had ripped him off, and I mean badly. If you can believe this, the buyer then bought the car at the other agency and now owned two nearly identical vehicles. Of course, the other rep told the buyer to scat back to our store and dump the vehicle in our lap and say, sorry, you can't win them all. The buyer was assured that our agency would let him out of the deal. And I probably would have if the credit hadn't been approved and the contract already cashed. As far as I was concerned, he was a proud owner. The nerve of the other dealer, attempting to pull such a dastardly deed; it really insulted my integrity and was a slap in our face. I could not stand for that. My boss would have held the customer to the contract as well.

Well, you guessed it! The other dealer did the same as we did, thinking that we would give in. The finance source approved both deals, reluctantly, because of the customer's good credit and the fact that both dealers did a tremendous amount of business with the lender. To conclude, the customer who thought he would sneak in the back door and improve his deal ended up the proud owner of his and hers automobiles. I wonder if he ever got married. At the time he was single and lived alone. I guess most people like to keep a spare car lying around. Did I hear you say that he could sell one? Oh yes, he tried, but the loss he would take was prohibitive. Many customers could walk in off the street and end up with the same car at a cheaper price through hard bargaining. The last I heard, he still owned 'em both.

The stories are endless

I could tell you horror stories for at least another week, but I believe you get the point. The really spicy stories are not suitable for print, and as a gentleman I could not tell them in mixed company. By now you are ready to spring into action. However, please do not put down the book as yet. Take just another minute to read the epilogue; it will give you some motivation. As a former sales manager, trainer, finance manager, and used-car manager who is used to giving pep talks at sales meetings, I certainly can't break up our little meeting without first getting you all fired up and primed to "rip off" a head or two, now can I?

. . . .

Now You Have As Much Firepower as Your Opponent, the Professional Automobile Salesman

Score one for the Gipper and become a "bottom buster"

If I were a coach and you were on my team, I would know beyond any doubt you were ready to go into the game and play first string. Why? Because you have it all. First of all, you have the knowledge to get the job done. As a matter of fact, after reading this book, you have as much knowledge as any veteran salesperson, and a lot more than the men and women who have been employed in the car business for only a year or two. If two people with the same knowledge compete, the person who will win is the one with the most desire. That brings me to my second point.

You must have the desire never again to get ripped off. The fact that you decided to purchase this book leads me to believe this about you. So you've got both knowledge and desire. Something, however, is missing: ability. Walter Payton didn't become the best rusher in the history of the National Football League by chance. He practiced and

117]

became a superstar. Chris Evert-Lloyd didn't become one of the world's premier tennis players just by showing up. She put in long hours of rigorous practice before she became one of the best. Pete Rose wasn't nicknamed "Charlie Hustle" because he waited for something to happen. The future Hall of Fame candidate probably took more than a few practice swings now and then.

So if you put your mind to it, and rehearse your lines, practice your acting ability, make good notes, and have a clear idea of your goals, then there is nothing in this world to keep you from making yourself a great deal on your next automobile purchase.

I want you to get such a smoking deal on your next car that the dealer will think you're a professional negotiator. Go out there and bust the hell out of a few "bottom lines." Then you may earn the right to be called a "bottom buster" and join the "BBC," the "Bottom Busters Club" of America. To qualify, just send me proof that you saved over one thousand dollars on the purchase of a new vehicle, and you're in. Send them in care of Macmillan Publishing Company, How to Outsmart the New Car Salesman, 866 Third Avenue, 5th Floor, New York, New York 10022.

Car Lingo and How to Use It

Who, what, when, where, and how?

Get ready to receive a brief education on the many terms, sayings, words, and phrases that are commonly used in the car business. You'll not only get a kick out of some of them, but you may find yourself getting angry if you recall some of them being used in a previous car deal you once did.

Everyone in the business uses this special language because it allows you to communicate a lot in a few words. For example, if I am talking to a colleague and he asks how I made out with my last "up," I can reply that I "tore his head off." In translation this means: on my last turn ("up") to talk to a customer I made a sale that gave me a great deal and a huge commission. But how can knowing the meaning of these terms ever help you when you are making a purchase?

You are sitting in the rep's office and he receives a phone call. If the caller is the manager or another sales pro, the rep's portion of the conversation might go something like this: "Yeah, I'll try it. I don't think it will be a problem. If I 'U A' the trade three, then I'll be brand new."

If you are going to be successful in the pursuit of a great deal, you must understand what is happening to you as it occurs. Here, " 'U A' the trade three" means that the

119]

rep is going to underallow your vehicle $300; that is, if your trade is worth $2000, you are going to receive only $1700 for it. They are in fact attempting to steal $300 from you. This happens most often when the vehicle you are buying is a hot seller. The dealer or managers will instruct the reps to accept no discounted deals and to steal as much money as possible on trade vehicles. This is called a "full gross deal," which is another way of saying that maximun profit is achieved. In a seller's market you can count on all dealers trying to wrangle a full gross deal out of you. Therefore, if you overhear " 'U A' the trade three," you just might be able to make it backfire in the rep's face.

If you listen to what is happening and understand it, then you'll certainly be a lot better off. And if you want to do a little intimidating on your own, just watch the expression on your rep's face when you calmly say, "Listen, 'pard,' I'm not a 'laydown' and I'm not a 'stroker,' but I just love a good game of poker, so if you plan to sell me this 'ride' you'd better think twice and not mess with my 'ACV,' my 'green,' or my pride!" If you make this little speech, be careful not to trip over your rep after he hits the ground.

Incidentally, the following car jargon can be hazardous to your health. The use of these terms and phrases on a regular basis may lead other people to believe that you too are in the car business. After studying this glossary you will be qualified to seek employment at dealerships everywhere. Have fun!

The Unabridged Car Lingo Glossary

ACV—"Actual Cash Value": the exact value of your trade vehicle, or the amount a dealer would pay if he purchased your vehicle off the street.

Additional Dealer Profit—Found on the supplementary sticker affixed to the window next to the "monroney labels." This occurs when the dealer needs to make money over and above the already high markup. Usually done to cars or trucks that move or get sold quickly and indicates pure greed on the part of the dealer.

Amount Financed—The amount of money remaining after tax, license, and selling price have been added together and the trade and cash down payment (if any) deducted. This balance represents what is owed to the dealer.

Appraisal—The value of your trade vehicle, determined by the dealer or the dealer's expert used-vehicle evaluator.

APR—The "annual percentage rate," or the rate of interest being charged each year to borrow money that is still owed on the vehicle.

As Is—Purchasing a (used) vehicle without warranty. "As is" means that there is no warranty on the vehicle either expressed or implied. You buy the vehicle as it sits and are entirely responsible for all repairs, even if the vehicle breaks down fifty feet outside the dealership.

Assumed Close—This occurs when a rep believes that you are going to buy despite all your statements to the contrary. The negotiations are over as far as the rep is concerned, and he simply pulls out a buyer's order and begins filling it out. If you do not veto his action, he will continue to write and you've just bought the vehicle. Some customers are just too timid to offer any resistance.

121]

The Bottom Line—The real picture, the lowdown, the nitty-gritty, the turkey without the dressing. In other words, the real cost of an item after every possible consideration.

The Bump—A smart manager will send the rep back to bump the deal as many times as he feels he can get away with it. For example, assume the rep comes from the manager's office with a counter-offer of $550 more than the customer offered. The customer may then agree to pay $250 of this $550. The rep must then consult with the manager. When the rep returns, the manager hardly ever accepts the customer's new offer; almost always he will be slightly higher. This difference is the "bump." If a manager bumped every deal over the course of a selling season just $75 and this dealer normally sold 2000 vehicles per year, then that dealer would enjoy an extra $150,000 in increased profit. Not bad for thirty seconds of work on each deal.

Buying Down Interest Rates—This occurs when the dealer and a bank get together to pull the wool over a buyer's eyes. If the normal rate that banks charge their own customers is 13 percent APR, they will let a dealer advertise (without using the bank's name, of course) a much lower rate, like 4 percent APR. The dealer, however, must assure the bank that all loans will be made at the going rate of 13 percent. Since no one gives something for nothing, the amount representing the difference between the bank's rate and the dealer's must be made up by adding it to the price of the vehicle. So a buyer could get a super-low interest rate and still end up paying a few thousand more for the vehicle. It is a no-win situation.

Capitalized Cost—This term (also known as the cap cost) simply means the selling price of a lease; that is, the agreed price you lease the vehicle for. Many lease reps tell customers that there are no discounts when leasing, that the customer must pay full sticker price. That statement is untrue. A lease is just like a purchase. Negotiate the price first, then figure the lease payment. Always get three or four lease-payment quotes. Lease charges will vary tremendously from dealer to dealer and lease company to lease company. Never accept a partial disclosure on a lease. Get all the facts before you sign, in writing.

Chiseler—A customer who doesn't believe the dealer price and will ultimately grind the rep into little pieces to get a deal.

Closed-end Lease—In this lease, the buyer assumes no responsibility for the vehicle at the conclusion of the lease except for abnormal wear and tear on the vehicle. This is commonly referred to as a "walkaway" lease. It is the only type of lease I can endorse because if the buyer takes care of the vehicle, he cannot get into trouble on the residual or end value of the lease. He will owe nothing at the end.

Closer—A person employed by the dealer to take over a deal from a salesperson and finalize it. That is, this person will be one of the better sales reps, one who can enter any situation and get the job done. Stated simply, the closer will close the sale . . . now!

Credit Union Sale—Usually a money sale or interest sale held by a credit union or group of credit unions in conjunction with special offers by dealers. In many cases the credit union will have a lot of money; in order to invest it for the members quickly, a sale will be held. This sounds good except that, in many instances, the special prices offered by the dealer are dubious. That is, a dealership may offer all cars in inventory at $99 over actual dealer invoice (which is great for the customer). Then the dealers will install a lot of costly options that do nothing but run up the price and the profit for the dealer. For example, if a paint protection package, which normally costs the dealer around $75 to install, is added to the vehicle, and the dealer charges $595 for it, then the dealer made a cool $520 in profit plus the $99 profit that attracted the buyer in the first place. I used to love these sales. Our profits were always much higher due to all of the dealer-added items that we told our credit union customers were not negotiable.

Dealer Ads—These are items that any dealership generally adds to a vehicle. Sometimes they are options that you can get at the factory, and sometimes they are services or chemicals which are added to improve the vehicle's appearance. If you see a long list of items added to a supplementary window sticker that will appear next to the big factory monroney label (required by federal law), then think twice before you enter into negotiations. These items are marked up greatly and do nothing but add more profit to the already high sticker prices.

Dealer Financing—At many used-car agencies and some new ones too, you may find that the dealer himself will carry a contract on a vehicle until it is paid for. There is nothing wrong with this except one thing. Most of the time when a dealer carries a contract, the buyer will not receive a credit rating from the dealer. The buyer trying to improve his credit standing will find it hard to do with a dealer unless that dealer reports to the local credit-reporting agency. Therefore, go to a bank to arrange financing if at all possible (except in cases where factory-sponsored financing is available at the dealer).

Dealer Prep—In nearly all cases the dealer prep charge is nothing but a way to increase profit. When the dealer's service people clean and service a newly delivered vehicle to make sure all is working properly, the manufacturer pays for some if not all of these charges. However, a few top-of-the-line dealers (the dealers who sell the most expensive cars) do perform special functions; in that case the charge, although always inflated, is justified. Never pay for dealer prep unless it can be verified.

Decap—Used in conjunction with leasing. Here, in decapping a lease, a buyer makes a cash down payment in order to reduce the cap cost or selling price. This decapitalization serves only to reduce the lease payments. On some occasions a bank or other funding source will not approve credit for a lease unless the lessee decaps. This is sometimes due to a lack of credit-worthiness or perhaps too many outstanding debts.

Demo Ride—Part of a well-planned sales presentation. It allows the customer to become acquainted at firsthand with the vehicle he intends to purchase. (See Chapter 3.)

Demonstrator—A dealer-owned vehicle that is driven as a company benefit by the dealer personnel. Ideally, these vehicles are well cared for and usually carry the same warranty as a new vehicle with no mileage. However, because some sales reps have abused this benefit, many dealers have dropped the company car program from their employee benefit package. Accidents and fender-benders as well as everyday scratches sometimes make these vehicles less than desirable. Before you buy a "demo" at any price, treat it as if it were a used vehicle. You'll avoid unpleasant surprises, such as needing an immediate oil and filter change, by nosing around a little.

Deposit—An amount of money that insures a vehicle will not be sold to anyone else for a specified period of time. In some cases a dealer will not even talk prices unless such "good faith" money is placed on a vehicle. In my opinion a deposit is not necessary in negotiating the price but is needed once the deal has been consummated and the papers signed. For a contract or purchase order to be binding, in most states a signature on a contract and money changing hands will suffice.

Depreciation—The amount a vehicle loses in value over time. To find out the depreciation, ask your banker for the residual value with regard to leasing. With this figure you will be able to calculate how much the vehicle you intend to purchase will be worth after a few years.

Double-Team Sales—In the larger car stores, two reps or a rep and a manager will often converge on you; one friendly and humble, one aggressive and hard-sell. They then begin to play on your emotions with a classic good guy–bad guy routine: the bad guy rep immediately takes charge, pushing you around, dictating what's best for you, and demanding answers to his leading questions. Meanwhile, the good guy's selling pitch is as laid-back as can be, and after enduring the other rep's harangue, you'll believe anything your friendly rep says.

Down Payment—An amount paid to reduce the amount to be financed and therefore the cost of the monthly payments. Most lenders will require 10 to 15 percent of the total selling price in cash or trade equity as a down payment. Many times a person's credit standing will dictate the amount of the down payment. If you have not paid too much, you can expect to recoup the down payment if you sell the vehicle at around the halfway mark of your sales contract.

Extended Service Contracts (Warranties)—An insurance policy to cover repairs of certain specified items should they fail. Practically every dealer offers some form of warranty. Be sure to read every word of the service contract you purchase, since it may contain a large deductible or else it may not cover all the parts. When the finance manager tells you how great the policy is, ask specific questions regarding the coverage. He may tell you that the engine is covered, but the coverage may not include parts that are not lubricated by engine oil. It will often seem easy to purchase a contract because you can pay for it by adding the price to your finance contract. Because this will increase your payments, ask for a quote with and without the policy. These service policies are good moneymakers for the dealers. Typically, a policy that will cost you four or five hundred dollars will produce a couple of hundred dollars of profit for the dealer.

Factory-Authorized Interest Rate—A rate offered by the factory as an inducement for buyers to purchase now. Make sure you get a "factory only" rate. Don't get confused with "buy down" rates.

Factory Rep—A person assigned by the factory to troubleshoot problems of customers and dealers alike. Separate service and sales reps handle your dealer complaints as well as complaints about the vehicle itself. A list of the reps in your area and how to get in touch with them is usually located in the back of your owner's manual; otherwise, your dealer can supply you with this information.

Flake—Commonly used in describing a customer who is either a poor credit risk claiming that he's a good one, or simply a buyer whose bark is worse than his bite. In any case, for the rep to have developed such an opinion, the customer must have earned it. If you gain such a poor reputation, your bargaining power will be reduced greatly.

Fleet Buyer, Fleet Department—Generally a company that usually purchases at least ten vehicles per year. Regular customers do not qualify for fleet discounts. In fact, if you are told that you've been given a "fleet deal," whoever is making the statement is pulling your leg. A fleet discount is nothing more than a price at which the dealer agrees to sell vehicles to companies in your area of the country, which is only a little more than the invoice price. In some cases, a rental or lease company will buy a car for as little as $25 over actual dealer invoice. Dealers with a big fleet business are generally the largest dealers in the community. Most agencies will have some sort of fleet department.

The Flip—This tactic is especially useful against a savvy customer, and you'll find yourself coming against it when you use the techniques in this book. The flip occurs when a rep or a closer who's been handling your negotiations suddenly turns you over to another rep, who resumes where the other left off. This indicates the first rep is losing ground to you in negotiations, and a more experienced or skillful rep is needed to get you back in line. Watch out! You've worked long and hard to establish control over your rep; don't throw it all away by accepting another salesman. Simply get up and demand your original rep. If they start making excuses, head for the door. You'll quickly see them agree to your demands at this stage rather than lose the sale.

The Grape—A customer who is considered to be an easy mark. This type exists more than you might think. For example, a customer who believes that the dealer gives no discounts and therefore pays full sticker price would be a grape. Or a customer who thinks his trade was only worth $5000 when it was really worth $7000 and boldly tells the rep that he won't trade for a penny under $5500 would also qualify for this dubious and costly honor. Don't make a mistake and shoot your mouth off about a subject you know very little about.

Hard Close—To make a sale some managers will pull out all the stops and send in three, four, or even five different people in an attempt to talk you into saying yes. It means you are doing a great job and are getting a good deal, but you'll need a massage and a steam bath afterwards. The tension's at a high level during a hard close because the grinders all have egos at stake, and the customer should eventually buckle under on the fourth or fifth try.

Hide the Keys—A tactic used to delay a customer's departure from the dealership. If a buyer is close to making a deal but is still a few hundred dollars away, a slick rep may conveniently lose the keys to the customer's trade for a few minutes in an effort to gain some valuable time. At the very least, the rep would be able to take another shot at his prospect.

Holdback—A "credit," usually 3 percent of the invoice amount, the car dealer receives from the factory after he sells and delivers a new vehicle to a fleet or retail buyer. This amount is credited to the dealer's open parts account and is considered to be extra profit on a financial statement. Only domestic car dealers receive holdback money.

Holding the Car—A dealer will tell you that he is holding a certain vehicle for you, and he may in fact do it. However, the only way to hold a vehicle while you are making up your mind is to place a deposit on it. This will usually mean that the dealer has an obligation to hold it for a specific time period.

Implied Warranty—Any time a rep or a manager says, even in a general conversation, "Don't worry, Mr. Smith, if you have a problem, I'll take care of it," you then have an implied warranty. If you have a witness to support your claim, this means that you could end up having a problem fixed that was not under any written warranty. It will seldom happen because most dealers include written disclaimers in all documents safeguarding them against such problems. But if you were promised as a part of the deal that certain things would be taken care of, then either get those promises in writing or have plenty of witnesses around as well as a good attorney. You might be in for a fight if you decide to make a claim.

Inventory Value—Some dealers will say during negotiations that they will bring out the inventory book and gladly show you the inventory value of a vehicle. This will be done so that you can see just how little the dealer is making. But inventory value is not the same as real invoice cost. The inventory card may have anything written down as cost, while the real invoice will have the exact price the dealer paid.

Invoice—The amount the dealer paid the factory for the vehicle. It will be an official form from the factory or division that produced the car and should not be confused with the inventory value.

Irate Customer—A loud, obnoxious individual who is shouting, cussing, and threatening everyone at the agency; but not for long. This person will be asked to leave or else will be escorted out by the police. There are rigid rules regarding how far a customer can go when he shouts or uses abusive language. Don't do it.

La Ha (Lah) Life and Disability Insurance—Commonly known as credit insurance, which will be placed on your finance contract if you so request. The finance manager will do his best to sell it to you since it does offer good protection, but at significant cost to the buyer. Look at the disclosure section of the contract to see the individual charge for each kind of coverage; then ask what your payments will be with and without the insurance so you can compare and decide.

Liner—A sales rep working for an agency that is controlled by a sales "system." This person's sole job is to greet the customer, point him toward a particular vehicle, offer a presentation and demonstration, and then turn the buyer to a closer. The liner makes no effort to discuss figures or prices. It is not his job.

Loaner—A fading custom. Due to high insurance rates, few dealers lend vehicles to customers any more.

Lop off the Customer's Head—Also known as tearing off the head, hitting a home run, killing the customer, murdering the customer, scoring a slam dunk. You get the drift.

Money Factor—Another way of expressing interest rates, used to calculate a payment. For example, 10 percent APR for a period of forty-eight months is said to have a money factor of .02547. To figure the payment on a $15,000 unpaid balance, multiply the balance by the factor: thus, $15,000 \times .02547 = $382.05 per month for forty-eight months with no credit insurance included.

Other money factors are:

Interest Rate/APR	Term (Months)	Money Factor
3%	36	.02912
3	48	.02216
4	36	.02957
4	48	.02262
5	36	.03003
5	48	.02308
6	48	.02355
6	60	.01938
7	48	.02402
7	60	.01986
8	48	.02450
8	60	.02034
9	48	.02498
9	60	.02084
10	48	.02547
10	60	.02134
11	48	.02596
11	60	.02185
12	48	.02646
12	60	.02236

NOTE: Never pay more than 12 percent APR on a vehicle purchase.

Monroney Label—The big factory label affixed to the passenger window of a new vehicle. By federal law, this sticker must appear on the window of cars only. The monroney label is not required on pickup trucks. Purchasing trucks that lack an MSRP or EPA fuel economy rating is like walking on the edge of a cliff. Sooner or later you fall off and get killed.

Mop and Glow Package—Another way of saying paint protection package or paint sealant package.

MSRP—Manufacturer's suggested retail price, also known as the sticker price, the window price, and monroney, it represents the price of a vehicle before any dealer-installed options are added.

Overallowance, Underallowance—Example: your trade vehicle is worth $2000 and you purchase a vehicle that sells for $12,000 but cost the dealer only $10,000 to buy. If he sells you the vehicle for $12,000 and gives you $2000 for your trade, how much profit does the dealer make? If you said $2000, you are correct. In the same example, if the dealer gives you $3500 for your trade vehicle, then he makes $500. If the dealer gives you more for your trade than it is worth, he is overallowing it by dipping into the profit. The more he overallows, the less his profit will be.

Using the same example, if your trade vehicle is worth $2000 and you receive only $1500 for it, the dealer has underallowed your trade and his profit is $2500. This is also called "stealing the trade." Don't let this happen to you.

Silence—After a rep has done all the talking and all the persuading possible and looks you in the eye and says, "Well, Mr. Smith, I've given you a good deal. How about buying right now?" and then shuts up, this is silence. The silence is so loud it's deafening; the next one who talks, loses. I myself have sat for as long as 19 minutes just staring at the customer as he tries to make a decision. After a minute or two the pressure becomes tremendous. If the rep makes a single sound, the whole moment is blown. Once you've presented your case, and you've done it well, there's no need to be redundant. The pressure is now on the customer, who possesses all the facts to make a decision.

Soft Sell—Many reps who sell vehicles without the use of a system have a nice easy manner. They tend to use finesse rather than a blackjack. However, these "real nice" people are just as deadly as a grinder, owing to their acting ability and power of persuasion. The friendly, warm, and thoughtful salesperson is not a tour guide at Universal Studios, but a professional who does this for a living. Be on guard; do not let your defenses down.

Splitting the Difference—A sales tactic with a high success rate. Once the buyer is close to making a deal, but a gap still exists between him and the manager concerning the price, one of the parties will nearly always propose to split the difference. If a manager offers you the opportunity to split the "D," turn it down. The offer would never be made in the first place if the store was making a small profit. Most of the time, when a split is offered by the store, the manager is simply trying to build even more profit into the deal. Don't compromise, for it is a sign of weakness on your part. Once you say you will pay a certain figure, stick to your guns. You'll finally get the deal you want. Some dealers will always be hungry for the business, even if you end up walking out and going elsewhere.

Stroker—A customer who wastes the rep's time, one who is just looking but has no intention of making a deal at any price. Don't do this because when you do want to buy, you'll find that managers and reps alike have good memories, especially if you have cost them a sale by taking up time during a busy period. If you need to look, do so when the agency is closed. Then you won't get a hassle or be hassled.

Sublet Work—If the dealership has booked too much work or if they are not equipped to do certain work, then they will farm it out. If this occurs, the dealer is responsible for the safety of your vehicle and must also stand behind the work or service performed by the sublet company. This is rarely a problem.

Supplementary Sticker—This is the small(er) window sticker that appears next to the big factory label on new cars. It lists all the charges (at retail prices) for dealer-installed items or options. The more options on this sticker, the higher the price and the profit margin become. Do not get confused. Sometimes the dealer may make this sticker look like the real factory label. If at the bottom line of the factory label you see the MSRP and then more charges, a supplementary sticker should be there, itemizing these extra charges. If not, complain loudly and demand one.

Switching—This occurs when a dealer advertises a particular vehicle at a super-low price. This "price leader" will attract many shoppers to the store. Often, however, when the buyer arrives with checkbook in hand to buy the advertised special, it is already sold. But, not at all coincidentally, the dealer does have another vehicle in stock priced somewhat higher (and usually loaded with a ton of dealer-installed items). "Switching" is unethical but legal in most states. Insurance laws generally prohibit insurance agents from switching and impose heavy penalties on those caught doing it. The same should apply to car dealers but does not. Be alert!

The Ten-Point Walk-Around—Used during a sales presentation, this is a ten-step approach to show you a vehicle completely. If a sales rep does not offer you such a presentation, you may want to ask for one because they can be very informative.

Three-Day Cooling-Off Period—Some customers think that when they make a purchase either by cash or by bank contract at a dealership, the law allows them time to come to their senses. Many buyers are confused by the so-called three-day cooling-off period some state laws provide. This, however, applies only if a person comes to your home and solicits your business there. All contracts and paperwork must be signed and completed at the home and not at the office. This means if the customer never sets foot in the car store, then he would have the right to cancel the contract within the three-day period. When you are buying a car, however, it is difficult not to go to the agency.

The Total Deferred Payment Price—I have seen customers actually faint when they see this figure on their contract. The total selling price, tax, license fees, dealer documentary fees, and total interest charge together equal the total deferred payment price. If you take the full length of the contract to pay it off, this amount represents your total out-of-pocket expenses.

Up System—An orderly method for salespeople to take customers as they come into the dealership. This way everyone gets a turn to sell. The opposite of the up system is the "open-floor system." Under this system, it is every man for himself and the survival of the fittest. A rep can take as many customers in a row as he wants and would be unconcerned whether any of his colleagues get an opportunity to speak to a customer. "Lot drops" occur where an open floor prevails. This is where you are talking to a rep and suddenly he's gone. You see him later talking to someone else. He dropped you because you did not answer the questions properly during the prequalifying period. If you say that you will not be purchasing for a couple of weeks, that is all it takes. On some occasions, when a rep is unable to lot-drop you because of a manager's keen eye, you can expect the rep to end the conversation quickly in order to move on to another person who may be in the market now.

Index

accent stripes, 17, 87, 88,
  103
actual cash value (ACV),
  69
  definition of, 121
additional dealer profit:
  definition of, 121
  See also dealer-added
    options
advertising:
  car-industry, xi
  choice of dealer and,
    44–45
AMC, 94
"amount financed,"
  definition of, 121
annual percentage rate
  (APR),
  definition of, 121
appraisal, 68–72
  definition of, 121
"as is" purchase, 121
"assumed close," 121

banks:
  and advance calculation
    of payments, 40
  dealers vs., as financing
    source, 123–124
  and decapping, 124
  and evaluation of trade
    vehicle, 42–43, 84
  preparation for dealing
    with, 39–44
  and upside-down buyers,
    110
  See also interest rates
black book, 42
BMW cars, 94
body language, 80
"bottom line," definition of,
  122
"bumping," 90–92, 95, 122
  by finance managers,
    107–109
"businessman" customers,
  27–28